MARRIAGE, SEPARATION, AND DIVORCE BRITISH COLUMBIA

MARRIAGE, SEPARATION, AND DIVORCE BRITISH COLUMBIA

Jane Auxier, LL.B.
Karen Nordlinger, Q.C.

Self-Counsel Press
(a division of)
International Self-Counsel Press Ltd.
Canada   U.S.A.

Self-Counsel Press acknowledges the financial support of the Government of Canada through the Book Publishing Industry Development Program for our publishing activities.

Printed in Canada.

First edition: November 1972
Tenth edition: August 1996
Eleventh edition: October 1998

Canadian Cataloguing in Publication Data

Auxier, Jane.
    Marriage, separation, and divorce British Columbia

    (Self-counsel legal series)
    First–2nd eds. by R. Flynn Marr, have title: B.C. family law and drafting marriage contracts; 3rd–8th eds., by Jane Auxier have title: Marriage and family law in British Columbia; 9th ed. has title: Marriage, separation, divorce, and your rights.
    ISBN 1-55180-218-X
    1. Domestic relations — British Columbia — Popular works.
    I. Nordlinger, Karen F.   II. Title.   III. Series.
    KEB194.Z82M37 1998   346.71101'5   C98-910796-5
    KF505.ZA4M37   1998

Self-Counsel Press
(a division of)
International Self-Counsel Press Ltd.
1481 Charlotte Road
North Vancouver, BC   V7J 1H1
Canada

1704 N. State Street
Bellingham, WA   98225
U.S.A.

CONTENTS

SAMPLES

NOTICE TO READERS

Laws are constantly changing. Every effort is made to keep this publication as current as possible. However, the author, the publisher, and the vendor make no representation or warranties regarding the outcome or the use to which the information in this book is put and are not assuming any liability for any claims, losses, or damages arising out of the use of this book. The reader should not rely on the author or publisher of this book for any professional advice. Please be sure you have the most recent edition.

In particular, the child support guidelines are a recent enactment and the case law is just emerging. They can be complex, depending on the financial situation of the parties, and the reader is urged to call the help line number shown in chapter 5 if he or she has any questions, or to consult with a lawyer.

INTRODUCTION

In recent years, our western culture has changed its emphasis from a sacrosanct preservation of the family as a unit to the individual independence of the members of the family.

The ease of obtaining a divorce (in comparison with the situation before 1968), the relaxation of stringent codes of sexual morality, the new status of women in society — all of these factors have caused both men and women to examine their roles as spouses more carefully and to sever the relationship in the family unit when circumstances demand it. Twenty years ago divorce was a stigma and problems in a marriage had to be tolerated; today, divorce is acceptable and problems of a serious and insoluble nature frequently result in the disruption of the family unit.

It is unfortunate that, despite our rapidly expanding sources of information, many individuals are unaware of the rights and obligations that arise from the separation of a husband and wife. A wife may contemplate separation or even divorce, but hesitate because her husband threatens to "cut her off without a cent." A husband may contemplate leaving his wife, but hesitate because his wife threatens to "take him for every penny he has" or to "make certain that he never sees the children again." Only on rare occasions do threats of this nature have any validity in law.

The purpose of this book is to acquaint you in general terms with the legal nature of a marriage and the consequences of a separation. If you have serious matrimonial problems, you should consult a lawyer.

1

HUSBAND AND WIFE

a. WHAT IS A MARRIAGE —
LEGALLY AND OTHERWISE?

During the last few thousand years of our cultural history, marriage and the extended family has been the basis of our social structure. ("Extended family" refers to the older family structure in which several generations and their relations by marriage either lived in the same dwelling or resided close enough to each other to still be considered one family unit.) And because these institutions have been entrusted with the care and raising of the children of our community, the state has always had a vested interest in every marriage and, for that matter, any other situation in which children are being reared, for the children are the one product on which the whole community depends for its existence.

Since before Roman times, marriage has been a matter of contract, at first between families, and later between the parties themselves. As time passed, the form picked up certain religious trappings, then state sanction, and, finally, today it comes to us encrusted and hoary with centuries tangled in its hair. But it is still basically considered a contract, not in the usually accepted sense possibly, but similar enough in form to be classed under that broad head of jurisprudence.

One legal writer has said,

> I have throughout treated marriage as a contract, because this is the light in which it is ordinarily viewed by jurists, domestic and foreign. But it appears to me to be something

1

more than a mere contract. It is rather to be deemed an institution of society founded upon the consent and contract of the parties; and in this view it has some peculiarities in its nature, character, operation, and extent of obligation, different from what belongs to an ordinary contract.

Once two people are married, the law takes on for them certain new aspects. Certain legal obligations arise between the parties themselves and between the parties and society as a whole. And, depending on whether or not these two people have entered into a legal marriage or what is commonly called a common-law marriage, society has a say in determining the type of relationship the parties will have.

The noble old institution does have its problems. For example, the law was never very precise about who does what in marriage, and does not provide a remedy when the parties are in dispute about how the marriage itself is to work. Years ago the problem was somewhat controlled because women really had no alternatives to consider. This is not the case today with so many women in the work force. The alternatives are now present, and both men and women are questioning their roles in marriage. In fact, many young people are questioning the whole institution.

The large extended family has disappeared and now we find the nuclear family, mom and dad, trying to do all of the tasks that once many hands pitched in to do. It is a heavy burden, and it tears at the resolve of the individuals involved. And with the mobility of our population we find people alone, away from the family, isolated, and cut off in a world that can be very hostile. The challenges from without tend to disrupt within. With the liberation of wife, the growing independence of children, the hard-sell good life thrown at dad, and a thousand other diversions, it is sometimes hard to keep clear the goals and the paths to those goals. All of these problems combined add up to a great pressure on every marriage relationship — so much so that we can well wonder what its future may be.

When two people do marry, the contract that they enter into is defined for them by law. They can also enter into a separate contract that sets out further principles — the so-called "marriage contract" — and this is discussed in another part of this book.

When two people enter into a common-law relationship, there are also certain principles of contract involved, although far fewer, and the obligations that common-law spouses incur toward each other tend to arise more directly from the provisions of the Family Relations Act. Rights and remedies between common-law partners tend to be a little more complex and are more likely to require the assistance of a lawyer should the relationship break down and require sorting out in the courts. The same can be said for same sex relationships.

b. DIFFERENCES BETWEEN FORMAL AND COMMON-LAW MARRIAGES

Once, long ago, marriage was not public in that it did not involve church or government. It was something composed wholly of tradition and the people; in other words, it was civil in nature. From about the tenth century on, the church became more and more involved, but valid marriages could still be entered into by contract as in the old way. The situation became chaotic as young people went off privately and, without telling mom and dad, formed valid marriages in secret. Eventually, about 1750, the government in England stepped in and passed a Marriage Act that set out how valid marriages were to be entered into.

The law in British Columbia does not sanction marriages not performed according to the provisions of the Marriage Act, but, of course, it does not prevent people from simply living together in the old way and so there have come to be "common-law marriages." These unions were for years outside of the law, and as the law of the family began to grow in the nineteenth century, the common-law union was ignored and the protections and benefits of marriage were not conferred upon it.

However, as more and more people in our society chose to live in this type of relationship, the legislature realized that these people also required the protection of the law, and sections of the Family Relations Act now reflect that. There is a recognition that in common-law unions, as in legal marriages, often the parties are not equal. One may have more training and skill than the other and be better able to find a good job. One may have the bulk of the obligation and emotional strain of raising children. And so one party becomes dependent on the other and certain rights and obligations arise. Should the couple separate, one may be required to pay support for the other and/or the children of the union or children brought into the relationship. The law in this regard is discussed in more detail in chapters 4 and 5.

Where the amount of support is concerned, the criteria are the same whether the parties were married or lived together. But there the similarity ends. The common-law or same-sex couple can end their relationship without court involvement, while the married couple must obtain a divorce.

c. THE FORMALITIES OF ENGAGEMENT AND MARRIAGE

The formalities of marriage in this province are governed by the Marriage Act. As already pointed out, this statute sets out the terms and conditions under which two people may marry and is very similar in form to the original Marriage Act passed in England about 1750.

Engagement is governed by the "common law." (The common law is age-old custom that has grown into formal law by being forged, piece by piece, in one reported legal decision after another.) Basically, an engagement is a contract to marry and is governed by the ordinary rules of contract. If one person breaks the contract, it may be possible to recover damages if the other can prove that damages were suffered as a result of the breach. This used to be a very popular form of action but is virtually extinct now.

As has already been mentioned, a marriage is a form of contract with certain implied terms conditional to it. Of these terms there are very few that the parties themselves can alter by their own will and desire. The formalities of the marriage as set out in the Marriage Act must be strictly observed. Basically, the Marriage Act sets out two ways in which the marriage contract can be concluded. One involves the church and religious ceremonies and the other is by way of marriage licence and civil ceremony.

Complications arise when very young people desire to marry. If under the age of 19, both persons require the consent of their parents, and should the parents not consent, the young couple may apply to a Supreme Court judge for consent. If both persons are under the age of 16, the consent of all parents is required, together with the consent of a Supreme Court judge. It is interesting to note, however, that once the marriage ceremony has been performed and the marriage has been consummated, even though the parties are too young, it may be a valid marriage. This would mean, for instance, that if you and your spouse are under 16 years of age, and you could complete the proper form of marriage and then consummate it, you would then be validly married.

Basically, the Marriage Act sets out the requirements for the registration of members of the clergy who may perform marriages and outlines the necessity for things such as marriage licences, witnesses to the marriage, and marriage certificates. No particular formal ceremony is described in the act and provision is made for both civil and religious ceremonies. In either case, the parties to the marriage are free to write their own ceremony if they can obtain the co-operation of the presiding minister or marriage commissioner.

d. WRITTEN MARRIAGE CONTRACTS

When two people say, "I do," they are in fact saying that they agree to abide by the terms of a contract written for them in law, for better or for worse, and whether or not they like it. Regrettably, the majority of people are not even aware of the existence or the contents of this agreement in law and very often find that some of the terms of this contract — either included or excluded — are so offensive to them that, had they known, they might have chosen not to marry.

In addition, when most people marry they are doing so with many assumptions about the nature of the relationship to which their partners may not subscribe. It is unfortunate that few people seem to sit down in advance and work all of these things out on paper. Apparently love does not question, which may be the reason that love is doing so poorly these days as a foundation for a marriage. It refuses to protect itself.

1. What kind of contract can you have?

Written contracts of marriage were once very common in England. This was especially so before the existence of the Married Woman's Property Act of the last century in England that gave women basic property and contractual rights they did not have before. Since the enactment of these statutes in England, and a similar statute in various Canadian provinces (the Law and Equity Act), marriage contracts fell into disuse, although they were still possible in law as long as they provided for the division of property during the marriage or upon death. Any provisions relating to separation or divorce of the parties would not be enforced because such contracts offended public policy. Certain limitations were placed on these contracts.

These limits come about because any marriage contract is really a three-cornered affair between the man, the woman, and the society, which imposes many of its own terms and conditions. To attempt to contract in any way that infringes upon these imposed terms and conditions would result in the courts striking down the offending provisions as being against public policy. Areas such as children, sex, permanence, and monogamy all have imposed terms.

Any attempts to contract, for example, that there be no children, that the parties remain celibate, that the marriage terminate after so many years, that there be more than one man and one woman in the relationship, or that there be any grouping of the sexes other than one of each kind would certainly be struck down in court. It is open to you to contract in any of these matters, but the courts will simply not assist you to support such a contract.

Since the introduction in British Columbia of the Family Relations Act, marriage contracts are undergoing a revival. The act embodies the concept of deferred community property: the idea that upon separation or divorce the parties will share equally in any property ordinarily used for a family purpose. The act does, however, allow you to contract out of this arrangement.

Under section 61 of the Family Relations Act, a couple may enter into an agreement, either before or during their marriage, in which they sort out the management of the family assets or other property during their marriage and determine the ownership in, or division of, family assets or other property during their marriage or in the event of separation or divorce. Duplex in my name since MAR.9 to this date. There was never a formal complaint on this matter. Therefore it is soley mine?

7

Apart from these matters, which are specifically mentioned in the legislation, a marriage contract may include items such as who is to perform the household chores, which parent is to have custody of the children in the event of a separation, what the support obligations will be, and so on. It is important to realize that not all of these provisions would be enforceable by the court. For example, the courts in British Columbia are the overseers of the welfare of children and private agreements do not negate their jurisdiction. Provisions for support are also not enforceable in a court if the amount set forth in the contract does not appear reasonable in light of respective incomes and expenses.

There is still great value to including provisions that could not normally be directly enforced by the court. Parties to a marriage seldom sit down and discuss how they expect the marriage to be conducted and how they see the responsibilities being divided. With more and more women entering the work force, more and more men have to face the task of sharing domestic duties. When things like house care and child care are all worked out in advance and set down on paper, there is a considerable psychological benefit.

First, you each get to know the other's views on these topics and have a chance to compare your spouse's views on marriage with your own. Second, if problems arise later on, the paper setting out the deal could carry great weight between you. And, finally, even though unenforceable directly, if you do end up in court in some dispute or other, the judge will be most interested in the agreement as an expression of the intentions of each of you. *Would it be desirable to forward intentions to BLS to show I mean good. (SA.T.P.)?*

Sample #1 shows an example of a pre-marriage contract and Sample #2 illustrates a marriage contract. The forms are not meant to be followed word for word. Rather, they are suggestions of what the agreement might say and look like. For each couple the terms will be different, reflecting the reality of the relationship the two people foresee. As an aid in drawing up such a contract yourself, a package of pre-printed forms, the *Living Together Contract,* is available from the publisher.

Should your intended spouse not wish to sign such a contract or come to any agreement about the intended relationship, you might consider whether or not you wish to go any further. Better the embarrassment of ending it now than the expense and heartache of legal action later. People who will not commit themselves to paper are not likely to commit themselves to you. And don't forget that although the relationship you have now will mature and change as you grow older, the chances of its maturing in the direction of an increasing commitment to helping and understanding one another are not very great. Before the marriage, you are at the height of co-operation; you may expect it to grow more remote in the future. If it is unsatisfactory now, think about bailing out.

2. The mechanics of writing a contract

All legal agreements have basically the same form, and once the form is mastered, any person can draw up an agreement that could be very useful, if not completely binding, on the parties that signed it. Basically, the document must encompass on its face the whole of the agreement entered into. This is because of a rule of law that states that a formal agreement becomes the whole agreement, unless it expressly says otherwise, and that any oral details that were agreed on and not included in the agreement go by the boards.

The agreement must show the date and place that it was written, the full names and addresses of the parties who signed it, and the terms and conditions set out in it. No legal language is necessary, but the words must be clear, precise, and have only one meaning so as to avoid possible future confusion. It must be signed by all of the parties it is to bind and should be

SAMPLE #1
PRE-MARRIAGE CONTRACT

THIS AGREEMENT made in quadruplicate this 2nd day of June, 199-.

BETWEEN:

> BETTY BLISS of the City of Vancouver,
> Province of British Columbia
> hereinafter called "the future Wife"

—AND—

> LARRY LONELY of the City of Vancouver,
> Province of British Columbia
> hereinafter called "the future Husband"

WHEREAS the parties intend to marry on or about the 4th day of July, 199- in the City of Vancouver, in the Province of British Columbia;

AND WHEREAS the parties have a clear understanding of the terms of this agreement and of the binding nature of the covenants contained herein; they freely and in good faith choose to enter into this marriage agreement and fully intend it to be legally binding upon themselves;

AND WHEREAS the parties hereto are desirous of determining their rights and duties during their marriage, upon death and in the event of marital difficulties to make such rights and obligations explicit so that fairness to all parties concerned may be facilitated;

AND WHEREAS each party is possessed of his or her own separate income and estate;

AND WHEREAS each party has been advised of the provisions and possible legal implications of the Family Relations Act, R.S.B.C. 1996, c. 128, and intend this agreement to be a marriage agreement within meaning of the act.

THE PARTIES AGREE AS FOLLOWS:

ARTICLE I
ASSETS AND LIABILITIES

1. The parties have made full disclosure to each other of all property and assets owned by each of them and of the income derived therefrom and from all other sources.

2. Each party shall during his or her lifetime keep and retain sole ownership, control and enjoyment of all property real and personal now owned or hereafter acquired by him or her free and clear of any claim by the other.

3. Notwithstanding any law or statute to the contrary, the parties hereto agree that they shall always be separate as to property.

4. The parties agree that those provisions of the Family Relations Act relating to family assets shall have no application whatever in the determination of ownership of assets of either party.

5. Neither party shall contract any debt in the name of the other, nor in any way bind the other for any debt for which either might in any way become liable. If either party shall at any time or times hereafter be called on to pay or discharge and shall in fact pay or discharge any debt or liability heretofore or hereafter incurred or contracted by the other, then, and in such case, the party making such payment, at his or her election and in addition to any other rights which she or he may have to recover same, may deduct and retain the amount which she or he shall have so paid out of any sum or sums of money then due or thereafter to become due to the other party; provided that she or he shall not pay any such debt or liability without first notifying the other party of the existence thereof and giving the other party an opportunity to pay it or dispute it.

6. The parties agree at all times hereafter each to keep indemnified the other, his or her heirs, executors, and administrators from all debts and liabilities heretofore or hereafter contracted or incurred by them, and from all actions, proceedings,

claims, demands, costs, damages, and expenses whatsoever in respect of such debts and liabilities or any of them, other than such as arise under this agreement.

7. Without in any way limiting the generality of the foregoing provisions, it is the intention of the parties to cohabit on the lands and premises municipally known as 123 Wedded Way, Vancouver, British Columbia, which lands and premises are owned by the future Wife absolutely. The future Husband agrees to remise, release, and forever discharge the future Wife from any right or claim which he may hereinafter acquire whether at law or in equity or under the provisions of any statute past, present, or future to the said lands and premises.

8. The parties acknowledge that the future Wife is the sole owner of all the contents of the lands and premises municipally known as 123 Wedded Way, Vancouver, British Columbia, and the future Husband shall not now or in future make any claim whatever against them.

9. In the event that the future Wife desires to terminate the marital cohabitation, the future Husband agrees to vacate the lands and premises municipally known as 123 Wedded Way, Vancouver, British Columbia, within a reasonable time after being requested by the future Wife to do so, and thereafter the future Wife shall be entitled to have exclusive possession of the said lands and premises.

10. The parties acknowledge that the future Wife is the absolute owner of the lands and premises municipally known as Lot 123, Whistler, British Columbia, which said lands and premises shall be available for the mutual enjoyment of both parties as a recreational vacation property during the period of their cohabitation. The parties further acknowledge that the future Wife is the exclusive owner of the contents of and the equipment contained in or about the said lands and premises. The future Husband acknowledges that he has not now nor will hereafter acquire any right, title, claim, or interest therein.

11. In the event that the future Wife desires to terminate the marital cohabitation of the parties, she shall notify the future

Husband and in such event the future Husband shall forthwith cease to be entitled to have the use or occupation of the said lands and premises at Lot 123, Whistler, British Columbia the contents of or the equipment contained therein and acknowledges that the future Wife shall have the right to exclusive possession thereof.

12. The future Wife acknowledges that the future Husband is absolutely entitled to the ownership of any chattels which he owned prior to the marriage and she shall not now or in the future make any claim whatever against them.

ARTICLE II
AFTER-ACQUIRED HOUSEHOLD GOODS

1. After-acquired household goods in this section includes furniture and effects used in or reasonably necessary to the running of the home which are acquired by either party subsequent to the marriage of the parties, but does not include purely personal items or goods used mainly by one of the spouses whether owned or otherwise.

2. The parties shall at all times be entitled to the financial contributions of either to the acquisition, maintenance, or capital improvement of the said household goods.

ARTICLE III
MOTOR VEHICLE

1. The parties acknowledge that they are each the owner of a separate motor vehicle.

2. The parties are equally entitled to the rights of use of both motor vehicles during their cohabitation.

3. Notwithstanding paragraph 2 hereof, either party shall be free to dispose of or otherwise deal with the beneficial title in the motor vehicle registered in his or her own name without the consent of the other.

ARTICLE IV
FINANCIAL OBLIGATIONS

1. Except as provided in this agreement, neither party shall be obligated to make any payment(s) of any kind whatsoever, directly or indirectly, to or for the benefit of the other and each party expressly renounces any right or claim which he or she has had, has, or may hereinafter acquire whether at law or in equity or under the provisions of any statutes, past, present, or future against the property, both real and personal of the other, now owned or hereafter acquired by him or her. Each party covenants and agrees that this agreement may be pleaded as and shall constitute a full defence and answer to any such claim and each party agrees that he or she will not at any time hereafter seek, ask, demand, or require in any manner or make any claims for monies or property, real or personal of any nature for himself or herself.

2. Neither party shall be obliged to make any payment or payments of any kind whatsoever, directly or indirectly, to or for the benefit of the other, and each party expressly renounces any right or claim which she or he has had, has or may hereafter acquire whether at law or in equity or under the provisions of any statutes, past, present or future for alimony, interim alimony, support, maintenance or otherwise and each party covenants and agrees that this agreement may be pleaded as and shall constitute a full defence and answer to any such claims and each party hereby agrees that he or she will not at any time hereafter ask, seek, demand or require in any manner or make any claims for monies of any nature for or toward his or her support and maintenance. Any Order or Judgment for alimony, maintenance or support shall be null and void between the parties, and if any such claim is made notwithstanding, the parties reserve their right to dispute the claims for any sum; and if any such Order is made notwithstanding, each covenants with the other to indemnify him or her and save him or her harmless for the effects thereof.

3. The parties agree that forthwith upon their marriage they shall open a bank account in both of their names at a mutually agreeable bank or trust company. The parties agree that they

shall each deposit into the said bank account in every calendar year the sum of $20 000 or such other sum as may be agreed upon by the parties from time to time provided that in any event each party's contribution to the said bank account shall be equal in any calendar year. The funds on deposit in the said bank account shall be used for day-to-day living expenses for the parties including but without limiting the generality of the foregoing, the household expenses and carrying charges for the lands and premises municipally known as 123 Wedded Way, Vancouver, British Columbia and Lot 123, Whistler, British Columbia, B.C. Medical Plan premiums, drugs, extra medical and dental care, club dues, entertainment, items of personal care, furniture re-placement, appliance repairs, and vacations. The funds on de-posit in the said bank account shall be held by the parties as tenants in common and each party shall have an undivided one-half interest therein.

4. If a dispute arises between the parties as to the use or disposition of funds on deposit in the said bank account, the parties shall attempt to resolve the dispute by mediation. E.L. Smith shall act as mediator. If he is unable to so act, the parties shall select an alternate mediator and, failing agreement, the future Wife shall select the mediator. The parties shall share equally the cost of mediation.

ARTICLE V
ESTATES

1. The future Wife releases and renounces all rights that she may have to the administration of the future Husband's estate in the event of the future Husband predeceasing her, and the future Wife renounces and releases the future Husband from any and all claims she has or may hereafter acquire against his estate under the Estate Administration Act or any other statutes or amendments thereto whereby a wife is or may be given a statu-tory claim against the estate of her husband.

2. The future Husband renounces all rights that he may have to the administration of the future Wife's estate in the event of the future Wife predeceasing him and the future Husband renounces

and releases the future Wife from any claims which he may hereafter have against her estate under the Estate Administration Act or any other statutes or amendments thereto whereby a husband is or may be given a statutory claim against the estate of his wife.

ARTICLE VI
VARIATION AND TERMINATION

1. This agreement cannot be varied or terminated at any time except by written agreement of both parties.

ARTICLE VII
CONTRACTUAL UNDERSTANDING

1. The parties to this agreement, while desiring this agreement to operate both as a guideline to their marital rights and responsibilities and as a legally enforceable agreement, understand that some clauses in this agreement may not be legally enforceable. Nonetheless, it is agreed that while the parties enter into this agreement as a whole, they also agree to enter into each separate provision of this agreement as if it were a separate agreement.

2. Each party to this agreement hereby confirms that the foregoing has been entered into without any undue influence or fraud or coercion or misrepresentation whatsoever and that each has read the herein agreement in its entirety and with full knowledge of the contents hereof and does hereinafter affix his or her signature voluntarily hereto.

3. The parties further covenant and agree to do and execute all further assurances and other instruments that may be required or necessary by either of them to give full effect to the terms contained in this agreement.

4. The words "the future Wife" and "the future Husband" are used in this agreement only to identify the parties. Except as otherwise expressly provided herein, no right or obligation herein created or reserved or imposed, shall cease to be impaired or affected in any way if the parties marry or the marriage between the parties is dissolved or annulled.

5. If the marriage does not take place, this agreement shall be in all respects and for all purposes null and void.

6. Each party hereby acknowledges that all matters embodied herein as well as all questions pertinent hereto have been fully and satisfactorily explained to them; that they have given due consideration to such matters and questions; that they clearly understand and consent to all the provisions herein; that they have been fully advised by their respective solicitors of their rights and liabilities; and that they are each entering into this agreement freely, voluntarily, and with full knowledge.

7. This agreement shall enure to the benefit of and shall be binding on the heirs, executors, and administrators of the parties.

8. The validity and interpretation of this agreement and of each clause and part thereof shall be governed by the law of the Province of British Columbia.

IN WITNESS WHEREOF the parties hereto have hereunto set their hands and seals.

SIGNED, SEALED AND DELIVERED
in the presence of:

Walter Witness
1234 W. 5th Avenue
Burnaby, British Columbia
Salesman

Walter Witness
_____
As to the signature of

Betty B Liss
_____
Betty Bliss

in the presence of:

Wilma Witness
1234 W. 5th Avenue
Burnaby, British Columbia
Homemaker

Wilma Witness
_____
As to the signature of

L Lonely
_____
Larry Lonely

SAMPLE #2
MARRIAGE CONTRACT

THIS AGREEMENT made in quadruplicate this 15th day of June, 199-.

BETWEEN:

MARY MATRI, in the City of Vancouver,
in the Province of British Columbia
(hereinafter called "the Wife")

OF THE FIRST PART

—AND—

MARTIN MATRI, of the City of Vancouver,
in the Province of British Columbia
(hereinafter called "the Husband")

OF THE SECOND PART

WITNESSES to the fact that the Husband and Wife (as the parties in this contract should be called) were married each to the other on the 10th day of May, 199-;

AND to the fact that the Husband and Wife have considered the present and future conduct and course of their marriage and have reached certain conclusions as to their relationship which they wish to have reduced to writing;

AND to the fact that the Husband and Wife wish to enter into a formal binding agreement with respect to the future marriage relationship and to be bound in law in that regard insofar as it is possible, and where the provisions of their agreement are not binding in law, to express their intention one to the other with respect to the matrimonial relationship they are attempting to develop and establish;

AND to the fact that although the marriage contract in its very nature is a contract for life, and is accepted as such by the parties hereto, that there do arise situations beyond the control of the parties hereto that make it inevitable that there be a separation of the parties and that the Husband and Wife wish to provide for that eventuality;

AND to the fact that each has disclosed to the other all of his or her estate, property, and prospects for now and the future and that each is fully conversant with the estate, property, and prospects of the other;

AND WHEREAS at the time of marriage, friends and relatives of both the Husband and the Wife gave marriage presents to each respectively which now constitute their separate property;

AND WHEREAS the Husband has been employed since the marriage and presently is employed as a plumber and receives $56 000 a year in wages;

AND WHEREAS the Wife has been employed for remuneration since the celebration of the marriage and has savings accumulated from that time in her own savings account and is now in receipt of a monthly child tax benefit;

AND WHEREAS the parties intend this agreement to be a marriage agreement within the meaning of the Family Relations Act, R.S.B.C. 1996, c. 128;

THE PARTIES AGREE AS FOLLOWS:

(From this point the same clauses used in the pre-marriage contract, starting with Article I, may be adapted for use in the marriage contract.)

witnessed. Witnesses should insert their full names, addresses, and occupations when signing the document.

These instructions are basic, crude, and approximate. If they cannot be followed, you should not necessarily give up on the agreement. Any written memorandum signed by both parties is of value or potential value in court. Conform as closely as you can, but get it on paper and have it signed. Even the very exercise of thinking it out will be of value in the long run.

The contracts shown in Samples #1 and #2 may have limited applications in court. In your life, it may be a good investment of a few hours of time to think out what it is that you, in fact, intend to do in the future. Spend time on your contract so that your final product reflects what you want, but try to follow the form and the brief instructions for completing it as closely as possible.

The agreements are short and tend to stay away from sweeping policy and philosophical statements. Very complicated provisions would only confuse the document should it ever have to be interpreted by a court. But expand as you will on the examples, keeping the wording simple, in point form, and understandable.

Make enough copies of any agreement so that each of you can have a signed copy for your own records. Keep your signed copy in a safe place, even away from your spouse, so that you are certain at least one copy will survive.

Having said all that, we should warn you that the courts are far less likely to enforce a contract when the parties have not received independent legal advice. For that reason, it would be preferable to thrash out the terms of an agreement with your partner and draft the document but then each seek legal counsel before signing.

3. Property agreements

Sometimes, people who have been married for some time wish to enter into a marriage contract solely to settle the property relationship between them. The form set forth in Sample #2 is an example of a marriage contract.

You should follow up the agreement by signing the necessary documents for filing in the Land Title Office so that its records conform to what the parties themselves have agreed to. A third party, such as a mortgage company, is entitled to rely on what the Land Title Office's records show. The third party would not be bound by any agreement to the contrary which the parties may have signed.

e. COMMON-LAW MARRIAGES — WRITTEN CONTRACTS

As mentioned earlier, couples who live in a common-law relationship acquire limited rights and obligations under the Family Relations Act. For example, the act embodies the concept that a husband and wife, upon separation or divorce, will share equally in any property ordinarily used for a family purpose. There is no equivalent law for parties who have never married. For this reason, a contract may be more important in such relationships. If you are agreed that you hold a joint interest in certain assets, obviously the best protection in cases of real property (land) is to have both names on the title. The same is true for items such as cars, boats, trailers, and other items requiring registration. Failing that, it becomes important to have a written contract setting out the intentions. It is possible for one common-law spouse to sue the other for an interest in assets under the law of "trusts." However, a contract will hopefully make this unnecessary.

2
SEPARATION AND SEPARATION AGREEMENTS

a. WHEN THE HONEYMOON IS OVER, WHERE DO I TURN FOR HELP?

When a marriage or other relationship between two people begins to disintegrate, you may wish to seek assistance by obtaining legal advice and/or some type of counselling.

1. Legal advice

Legal advice is important for protection because of the changing and sometimes ambiguous situation that may exist. Unfortunately, consulting a lawyer tends to be considered an aggressive rather than conciliatory step and may have a negative influence on your chances of getting together again.

If you wish legal advice but still intend to make a serious attempt at reconciliation, you should either fully disclose to your partner your intent to seek legal advice and seek the partner's approval, or the legal advice should be sought in complete secrecy. Legal advice should never be used as a lever as then it will only aggravate whatever relationship still exists.

When you consult a lawyer for purposes of merely seeking advice, not wanting to further disrupt an already troubled marriage relationship, make very clear to the lawyer that you still wish to keep open all possible channels for reconciliation. The lawyer should be very carefully instructed to take no steps that could be damaging to this end and, possibly, to do nothing until you have had further opportunity to explore the situation.

2. Other counselling

Even if legal advice is sought, however, it is frequently wise to obtain some type of counselling. This can be related to two specific goals: either reconciliation (getting back together again) or conciliation (trying to sort out the problems with a minimum amount of difficulty and dispute).

Counselling may well serve to save a disintegrating relationship. It is sometimes surprising what a difference the independent views of a third party can make in such a situation. Even if you and your spouse have passed the point of wanting to save the relationship, counselling may well assist you to end your unhappy marriage with less social, psychological, and economic costs. There are a growing number of professionals entering the arena of mediation including doctors, lawyers, social workers, and psychologists.

These various services are sometimes difficult to locate and perseverance may be necessary to establish contact. In many cases, one party is willing to see a counsellor but the other is reluctant. One party may have gone beyond the point of caring or may have withdrawn into a total "self-first" attitude. If so, it is likely too late for any amount of counselling to be of assistance. At this point, the other partner should refer quickly to the later chapters of this book for advice.

3. Financial problems

Financial problems can be of considerable difficulty for a family and put tremendous pressure on the marriage relationship. In such a situation, a local banker might be able to offer useful advice or, if not, recommend someone who could.

4. Mental health problems

If there is a problem involving mental disorder or breakdown, doctors and psychiatrists are available — in private practice or as part of a community care team. Access to such help is easily obtained by a referral from your family doctor.

If, despite the advice and counselling referred to above, the matrimonial problems continue, the parties may have to face the prospect of separating and living apart. What then?

b. WHAT IS A LEGAL SEPARATION?

The term "legal separation" is meaningless in British Columbia law. A husband and wife are legally separated when they live separate and apart from each other.

However, when a husband and wife separate, there are certain rights that each may assert and corresponding obligations that each may be called upon to fulfil. The assertion and enforcement of these rights and obligations can be done either through mutual agreement or by adjudication in the courts.

These rights and obligations may involve not only the spouses, but also the children of the marriage. The most frequent issues arising between husband and wife can be categorized as follows: custody, access, and support of children; maintenance of the spouse; title and possession of property; and divorce. Each of these categories is more thoroughly dealt with in succeeding chapters of this book. A court may deal with each type of problem separately or combine some of them in one court action. It is not necessary for a spouse to apply for a divorce before asserting one of these claims.

If neither spouse wishes to make a "claim" against the other, they merely have to establish separate residences to become "legally" separated. This type of "clean break" happens infrequently. In the majority of cases there are at least some rights and obligations that must be either agreed upon or settled by the courts.

c. SEPARATION AGREEMENTS EXPLAINED

At one time it was the law that one spouse could take action in the courts to force the other spouse to live with him or her. This, in effect, was an enforcement of one of the unwritten terms of the marriage contract. However, such an action has been abolished.

The law as it now stands is that two people, whether they are married or not, who have lived together by consent for any length of time can separate at any time merely by one or the other deciding to move out. It is that simple and there is no legal requirement that the parties move back in together. The separation is legal. There may be strings that one person has on the other such as children, property, or money, and which person moves out first may have considerable legal implication, but that does not affect the fact that the separation itself is legal.

Having said that, we must add that the court certainly looks beyond the question of *who* moved out to find out *why* he or she moved out. Many people are afraid to make the break, even though it's certainly justified by their circumstances, because of the fear that they will automatically be viewed by the court as the "bad guy." Not so.

The exact nature of the relationship that one party has with the other after the separation depends on the individual circumstances of the separation and on the legal status of the parties with respect to each other and their conduct leading up to the separation. All of these matters are discussed later in this book.

When parties do separate, or are in the process of planning their separation, they can enter into a contract, which is really just a written agreement setting out the terms and conditions under which they are separating; things such as who gets the car, the kids, the house, and the debt payments are sorted out on paper. Lawyers refer to such documents as separation agreements. They are usually drawn by a lawyer but this isn't necessary and any document drawn and signed by the parties will have value.

As stated before, the courts are much more inclined to enforce such an agreement if the parties have had separate legal counsel. Thus, ideally, the separation agreement should be drawn by a lawyer and one party should sign in front of that lawyer, the other party in front of a separate lawyer so that each gets independent advice on the true legal effect of the action. Separation agreements are legally very powerful and should not be entered into lightly. An example of a typical separation agreement is shown in Sample #3.

No one can be forced to sign a separation agreement and, should that happen, a court will rapidly overturn the agreement and reconsider the whole situation. An agreement that both parties can live with is frequently preferable to an enforced settlement on the basis of legal rights and duties.

As with a marriage agreement, a separation agreement can provide for the ownership and division of property, support obligations, the right to direct the education and moral training of the children, and any other matter required in the settlement of affairs. The contract can specifically provide for the custody of, and access to, children and generally the court will enforce this provision unless it is contrary to the best interest and welfare of the children. The contract can also provide for who is to have the right to live in the matrimonial home.

Should you ever be in a position of wanting to change the terms of a separation agreement, you will require the advice of a lawyer. One final point here: getting an agreement changed is difficult, so, before signing, make sure it says what you want it to say and covers all the relevant points.

SAMPLE #3
SEPARATION AGREEMENT

THIS AGREEMENT made in triplicate this 27th day of June, A.D. 199-

BETWEEN:

> JACK JAMES SPLITUPP, Carpenter, of 5555
> 55th Street, Wilton, British Columbia
> (hereinafter called "the Husband")

OF THE FIRST PART

—AND—

> JUDY JILL SPLITUPP, Housewife, of 1293
> 68th Avenue, Wilton, British Columbia
> (hereinafter called "the Wife")

OF THE SECOND PART

WHEREAS the parties hereto are Husband and Wife and were married on the 4th day of August, A.D. 199- at Vancouver, British Columbia;

AND WHEREAS the parties hereto have two children, namely:

JILL SPLITUPP, born in Wilton, British Columbia, June 24, 1989;

ROBERT SPLITUPP, born in Wilton, British Columbia, December 20, 1995;

AND WHEREAS the Husband and the Wife have agreed to live separate and apart and did commence to live separate and apart, on or about the 1st day of September, A.D. 1998 upon terms and conditions hereinafter expressed;

AND WHEREAS each party is fully advised and fully informed of the estate and prospects of the other party and the parties have been severally advised and informed by their respective solicitors of their respective rights and liabilities against and to each other and with reference to the property and estate of each other;

AND WHEREAS the parties desire to provide for the orderly settlement of their affairs and their respective rights and obligations upon separation and subsequently upon dissolution of the marriage or upon death as particularly set out herein;

THE PARTIES AGREE AS FOLLOWS:

1. THE PROPER LAW of this contract shall be the law of the Province of British Columbia, and this contract shall also be deemed to be valid and enforceable in accordance with the law of any other jurisdiction. The parties intend all of their affairs and property to be governed by this contract and the law of British Columbia, and, without restricting the generality of the foregoing, jointly and severally declare that the contract provides each spouse with the interest in each family asset to which he or she is entitled upon marriage breakup, as provided for in the Family Relations Act, R.S.B.C. 1996, c. 128.

2. THE PARTIES will, during the currency of this agreement, live separate and apart from each other as though each were unmarried and each will henceforth be free from the control and authority of the other, and shall reside and may reside at such place or places and in such manner as he or she shall see fit, and may work at any employment or carry on any business as he or she may see fit or proper, and shall not at any time hereafter require the other to live with him or her, nor shall either party institute any legal proceedings against the other for restitution or conjugal rights or molest or annoy or interfere with the other in any manner whatsoever.

3. IF AT anytime during the currency of this agreement the Husband and Wife shall by mutual consent agree to cohabit as Husband and Wife then and in such case this agreement shall become null and void and of no further effect; PROVIDED THAT, resumption of cohabitation during any period of not more than ninety (90) days, when such cohabitation is resumed or continued with reconciliation as the primary purpose, shall not compromise this agreement and it shall remain in full force and effect.

4. THE HUSBAND agrees that the Wife shall have, forthwith after execution hereof, full custody of the infant children of the marriage, namely, JILL SPLITUPP and ROBERT SPLITUPP, above described; PROVIDED THAT the Husband shall have generous access to the said children, such rights of visitation to include overnight, weekends and vacations by prior arrangement with the Wife; PROVIDED FURTHER that the children shall, by prior arrangement and with the consent of each child spend Easter, Christmas and summer vacations with either of the parties and neither of the parties shall unreasonably withhold consent to such vacation

visits; AND FURTHER PROVIDED that such visiting and vacation provisions may be varied from time to time as the children reach certain ages where they, or either of them, can reasonably be removed from the care and control of the Wife for periods of time consistent with the state of her or his development, health and general well-being, consent to which proposed variations shall not be unreasonably withheld by the Wife.

5. EACH OF THE PARTIES hereto agree that if the Wife either dies or becomes physically incapacitated and unable to care for the children of the marriage, then custody of the children of the marriage shall revert to the Husband.

6. THE WIFE and Husband agree that they shall have joint responsibility for making decisions with respect to the education, including choice of schools; health care, including choice of doctors, dentists, and surgeons; summer plans, such as the choice of camps and trips; and the general welfare of the children, and reserve the right to be consulted with respect to each or all of the foregoing.

7. THE HUSBAND and Wife each agree that the children may be removed from the place where they are to reside, for a visit with the Husband, but if the children are to be removed from the Province of British Columbia, they, or either of them, may only be removed by prior agreement of the Wife and upon the undertaking of the Husband to return them, or either of them, to the possession of the Wife at the residence of the Wife, as it may be from time to time.

8. THE WIFE agrees to continue to reside with the children in the City of Wilton, Province of British Columbia, for the purpose of giving full effect to the access provisions of clause 4 above; PROVIDED THAT if it becomes necessary for the Wife to move out of the City of Wilton to other places within the Province of British Columbia for the purpose of seeking or maintaining suitable employment, the Husband will not unreasonably refuse to agree to such relocation as may be necessary from time to time.

9. THE HUSBAND and Wife agree that in the event of serious illness of the children, or either of them, each will give the other prompt notice of such illness, but that the party in whose custody the child is at the time of such occurrence may, without reference to the other, arrange for emergency care.

10. THE HUSBAND and Wife covenant and agree, from the time of commencement of this agreement, to be jointly responsible for the payment of all and whatever is necessary for the support and education of the children of the marriage, regardless of where they may be resident from time to time, and neither remarriage nor commencement of cohabitation by either or both of them with a third person will relieve them of this responsibility; PROVIDED THAT such payments for the children, or either of them, are to continue until the respective child reaches the age of nineteen (19) years, unless he or she sooner marries or leaves school, in either of which events the support payable by the Husband and Wife shall, at the option of either the Husband or the Wife, cease; AND PROVIDED ALSO that if the children, or either of them, continue his or her education beyond the age of nineteen (19) years, such payments for support shall continue in respect of the children, or child, until the education to the first post-secondary school certificate or degree is completed in a timely manner.

11. THE HUSBAND covenants and agrees that he will provide to the Wife the sum of $XYZ per month for the support of the children of the marriage for so long as child support is payable pursuant to the Divorce Act, 1985 and pursuant to the Federal Child Support Guidelines.

12. THE HUSBAND covenants and agrees that he will pay to the Wife for her maintenance and support during the period of time in which she is completing her education at the University of British Columbia the sum of $XYZ per month and thereafter will continue to pay the sum of $XYZ per month until she finds employment or for a period of three (3) years or until divorce, whichever is the soonest.

13. THE HUSBAND covenants and agrees that he will, for the purpose of giving full effect to paragraphs 6 and 10 above, make additional payments with respect to the maintenance and support of the children of the marriage, which from time to time may be appropriate as a result of: emergency; medical, dental and surgical expenses, hospitalization and the like; and, with respect to the tuition of the children, or either child of the marriage, who may be a worthy candidate for college or university education.

14. THE HUSBAND covenants and agrees to maintain health insurance coverage including medical, hospital, surgical coverage and to pay for such items as eyeglasses and prosthetic

devices as and when required, only on behalf of the children of the marriage, in specific fulfilment of his responsibilities for performance of these provisions of the Agreement, and to maintain such coverage with respect to the Wife until she becomes employed or until she is no longer qualified, for whatever reason, to be included under the insurance plans available to him through his employer.

15. THE HUSBAND covenants and agrees to pay the cost of all necessary dental care for the children of the marriage PROVIDED THAT a Dental Insurance Plan is available at the Husband's place of employment. THE HUSBAND COVENANTS AND AGREES to take and maintain dental insurance coverage with respect to the children of the marriage in specific fulfilment of his responsibilities for performance of this provision of the Agreement, and to maintain such coverage with respect to the Wife until she becomes employed or until she is no longer qualified, for whatever reason, to be included under the insurance plans available to him through his employer.

16. THE HUSBAND AGREES that he will support the children to the extent set out above as well after as before divorce and that the support terms of the agreement are to be binding upon his executors, heirs and assigns.

17. THE HUSBAND AGREES to permit the Wife and children to have possession and occupancy of the matrimonial home at 1293 68 Avenue, in the City of Wilton, Province of British Columbia, more particularly known and described as,

City of Wilton
Lot 52
Block 28
District Lot 2027
Plan 1584

without requiring the payment of occupational rent, for the same period of time during which she receives the sum of $XYZ per month for her own maintenance and support as set out in clause 12 above.

18. THE HUSBAND AND THE WIFE covenant and agree that the Wife holds title to the matrimonial home in her name alone upon a resulting trust with respect to one-half undivided

interest for the Husband; AND THE WIFE AGREES that when she is no longer entitled, pursuant to the provisions of clauses 12 and 17 above, to occupy the matrimonial home without payment of occupational rent that she will do all things necessary, in concert with the Husband, to expeditiously sell the house; AND THE HUSBAND AND WIFE AGREE that the net proceeds from the sale of the matrimonial home at the above-noted future time will be equally divided between them.

19. EACH OF THE PARTIES AGREES, that in the event of the death of either of the parties the interest of that party in the fee simple with respect to the matrimonial home, whether vested or in expectancy, will pass to the surviving party as though the parties were registered as joint tenants, and as though this Agreement did not exist, for so long as this Agreement is executory; AND EACH FURTHER AGREES that when the time set out in paragraphs 12 and 17 above has run, the fee simple in the matrimonial home shall vest in them as tenants in common and until the matrimonial home is sold and the net proceeds have been distributed, each shall be free to dispose of his interest by sale, or, upon death, by testamentary disposition or, in the event of intestacy, as provided in the Estate Administration Act, R.S.B.C. 1996, c. 122.

20. THE WIFE covenants and agrees to make all of the monthly payments on the mortgage on the matrimonial home including principal, interest and taxes; AND THE WIFE FURTHER agrees to indemnify and save harmless the Husband from any liability however arising from the mortgage on the matrimonial home presently standing in her name as the mortgagor, and without limiting the generality of the foregoing to save him harmless from any claim whatsoever against him as guarantor of the first mortgage against the matrimonial home.

21. THE WIFE covenants and agrees to pay for all current and routine maintenance required, from time to time, to keep the matrimonial home in proper trim and repair and to pay all costs incurred for those purposes.

22. EACH OF THE PARTIES agrees that in the event any improvements or alterations are to be made to the house that neither party will have the right or privilege of committing the other to the payment of any costs incurred but both parties agree that the costs of such alterations and improvements may be

negotiated between the parties PROVIDED THAT neither party shall be under any obligation to consent to payment of all or part of the cost of any such alterations or improvements.

23. EACH OF THE PARTIES agrees that the matrimonial home may be sold and the net proceeds divided equally upon any one of the following occurring:

(a) If at any time both Husband and Wife agree to the sale of the matrimonial home, notwithstanding any other provision in this agreement;

(b) If the Wife, for any reason, voluntarily vacates the matrimonial home for a continuous period of more than thirty days; or,

(c) If the Wife permits the mortgage to fall into arrears and does not bring it into good standing within thirty days of the default, upon the occurrence of any of which events the Husband will be excused from further performance of his promises under Paragraph 17, above, and the WIFE AGREES that the Husband may, at his sole option, register the quit claim deed with respect to a one-half interest in the matrimonial home, which the Wife will provide to him upon execution of this agreement.

24. THE WIFE AND THE HUSBAND covenant and agree to co-operate each with the other in offering the matrimonial home for sale when it becomes available for sale under the terms of this agreement; and each of the parties further agree to execute all documents necessary for the listing and sale of the matrimonial home pursuant to this and other clauses in the agreement at their own separate costs and expense and to instruct their respective solicitors to enter into appropriate undertakings between solicitors to ensure the full protection of the respective interests of the husband and of the wife under this agreement.

25. THE HUSBAND covenants and agrees to make all payments and assume all obligations of the marriage incurred up to and including the date of separation and, without limiting the generality of the foregoing, to pay all bills including up to the date these presents including any charges incurred by way of credit card by either Husband or Wife, and the Husband agrees that he will keep the Wife indemnified therefrom and save harmless the Wife from and against all liabilities hereinafter contracted or encountered by the Husband and all claims,

actions, and demands on account thereof and all costs, charges, damages, and expenses to which the Wife may be put by reason of, or on account thereof.

26. THE WIFE covenants, at all future times, to keep the Husband indemnified against all debts and liabilities hereinafter contracted or incurred by the Wife, against any and all action or actions, proceedings, claims, demands, costs, damages and expenses whatsoever in respect thereof, and will not pledge the credit of the Husband, and if the Wife incurs any additional debts, whether for NECESSARIES or otherwise, while the Husband is not in default under the maintenance and support clauses of this contract, the Husband is to have the right to reduce the payments to the Wife by the amount he has to pay with respect to those debts.

27. THE WIFE shall not continue to be a beneficiary of any existing policy of life insurance on the life of the Husband, which insurance the Husband binds himself to maintain in force for the benefit of the children of the marriage and with respect to which he assigns all his right to the said children, AND the Wife covenants and agrees that she will do all things necessary to delete her name as beneficiary from the policy currently in effect on the life of the Husband, and shall and does, save as herein stated, hereby release to the Husband all and any interest she has, or may otherwise have obtained, in the existing or any future policy of insurance on the life of the Husband.

28. THE HUSBAND hereby releases to the Wife all and any interest he may otherwise have obtained in the existing or any future policy of insurance on the life of the Wife.

29. THE HUSBAND shall be absolutely entitled to:

(a) All his personal clothing, jewellery, and effects wherever situate;

(b) 1997 Volkswagen, registered NJA 924;

(c) One-half interest in an Erickson 27-foot Watership I Boat subject to a mortgage against it in the amount of $14 000, with respect to which debt he shall be solely responsible;

(d) Stocks and bonds currently in his possession or standing in his name;

(e) All the power tools and equipment in and about the matrimonial premises and,

(f) One deep freeze unit and one vacuum cleaner, each of which is to be selected by the Wife.

30. THE HUSBAND acknowledges that he has received from the Wife all his chattels and effects and any chattels and effects in which he may have any right or claim, and without limiting the generality of the foregoing, including everything set out in the paragraph next above.

31. THE HUSBAND acknowledges that he is to pay all insurance premiums with respect to the house, the household contents, the boat, the automobile, and all other personalty in his possession, pursuant to this agreement.

32. THE WIFE shall be absolutely entitled to all her personal clothing, jewellery, and effects wherever situate, all furniture, furnishings, fixtures, equipment, silverware, and household effects in or about the matrimonial home or in storage as at the date of this agreement and the Husband hereby releases and quits claims to the Wife any right, title, or interest which he has or may have therein, except as otherwise provided in clause 29 of this agreement.

33. THE WIFE acknowledges that she has received from the Husband all her chattels and effects and any chattels and effects in which she may have any right or claim and, without limiting the generality of the foregoing, including everything set out in the paragraph next above.

34. THE HUSBAND AND WIFE agree that each has his or her own separate bank account and that the other is entitled to the contents of the bank account or accounts held in their names and each hereby relinquishes any claims he has or may have with respect to the account of the other, wherever those accounts may be situate.

35. THE PARTIES hereto for themselves, their heirs, executors, administrators, and assigns, that they will, from time to time and at all times hereafter upon such reasonable request and at the costs of the other of them, his or her heirs, executors, administrators, or assigns, execute and do all further assurances and acts for

the purpose of giving full effect to these presents herein contained.

36. EACH OF THE PARTIES hereto renounces and relinquishes all right, title, and interest in the estate of the other and all right to participate in, benefit from, or administer the estate of the other;

37. SUBJECT TO the provision of this agreement, the Wife hereby releases the Husband from any action that she now has or may have against the Husband for support, maintenance, interim alimony, permanent alimony, or otherwise for herself.

38. NOTHING in the agreement shall prevent either of the parties from taking or instituting proceedings for divorce as they may be advised according to law on the ground of conduct that may have occurred previous to the date of these presents.

39. EXCEPT as otherwise expressly provided herein, no right or obligation herein created, reserved, or imposed shall cease, or be impaired, or affected in any way if the parties are divorced; and THE TERMS of this agreement are to survive a subsequent divorce and are to be enforceable as though the parties hereto were still married.

40. EACH OF THE PARTIES to this separation agreement covenants and agrees that the provisions of this agreement shall survive the occurrence of any and all events that have occurred or may in the future occur under Section 61 of the Family Relations Act, or upon death, insofar as the provisions relate to an orderly settlement of the distribution of property.

41. THE WORDS "Husband" and "Wife" are used in this agreement only to identify the parties.

42. WHEREVER the singular or masculine is used throughout this agreement, the same shall be construed as meaning the plural or the feminine where the context or the parties hereto so require.

43. AND IT IS EXPRESSLY AGREED between the parties hereto that all covenants, provisos, and agreements, rights, powers, privileges, exclusions, and liabilities contained in this agreement shall be read and held as made by and with and granted to and imposed upon the respective parties hereto and their respective heirs, executors, administrators, successors, and assigns, as if the words heirs, executors, administrators, successors, and assigns had been inscribed in all proper and necessary places.

IN WITNESS WHEREOF the parties hereto have executed this agreement as of the date first above written.

SIGNED, SEALED, AND
DELIVERED BY JACK JAMES SPLITUPP
in the presence of:

I. M. Witness

_____

SIGNED, SEALED, AND
DELIVERED BY JUDY JILL SPLITUPP
in the presence of:

Susy Que

_____

1. What value is a separation agreement and can it be enforced?

It is often heard that separation agreements are of no value. Equally, one frequently hears that the law is of no value. This is because the law — and separation agreements — are like hammers. A hammer on a workbench will not get up and drive nails for you. You have to pick it up and use it. The law is the same; it is a tool to be used, and if the separation agreement is being broken by your spouse, the law will not jump in and enforce it for you. You must take up the law and use it to enforce your rights.

The advantages of having a separation agreement are numerous. First, the existence of a separation agreement is an incentive to avoid litigation. It is always preferable to settle your disputes as quickly and as painlessly as possible. If you get involved in litigation, the results may be unpredictable, the procedure lengthy, the emotional trauma considerable, and the expense substantial.

Second, if you are making payments for the support of your spouse, you may deduct these payments from your gross income to compute your taxable income. The payments made are then included in the income of the recipient for income tax purposes. In order for this to apply, the following conditions must be fulfilled:

(a) The payments must be made to your spouse directly, or to a third party with the consent of and for the benefit of your spouse (e.g., payments to the landlord for rent). Note that these third party payments will be treated as child support *unless* they are clearly identified as being solely for the benefit of the spouse.

(b) The payments must be for the benefit of the spouse.

(c) The payments must be periodic; a lump sum, even though it may be payable in instalments, is not deductible.

(d) The payments must be made pursuant to a written separation agreement or an order of the court.

(Please note that *child* support payments are *not* tax deductible unless they were ordered or agreed to prior to May 1, 1997. This issue is discussed further in chapter 5.)

A third advantage of separation agreements that must be considered is that courts are bound by certain rules and there are only certain kinds of orders they can make. On the other hand, parties entering into a separation agreement are free to contract for almost any form of settlement that they think fit. In other words, they can enter into types of arrangements that the courts would not want to order and so a separation agreement has greater flexibility and potential convenience for the parties concerned.

However, unless the agreement specifically provides for review, it may stand in the way of further court action regarding spousal maintenance unless the circumstances have radically changed from the date of signing of the agreement and were unforeseen at that time.

Last, the date a separation agreement is signed is important when there is matrimonial property to be appraised and divided. British Columbia does not have true community property laws in which both spouses share equally in family assets *throughout* their relationship. Rather, there is "deferred community property." Simply put, this means a husband or wife is entitled to a one-half interest in each family asset after the relationship ends (i.e., when a separation agreement is signed or a divorce is granted). The date is important because of the fluctuation in value of family assets, especially real estate. For example, if a couple sign a separation agreement in November, 1994, but don't actually divide their assets until November, 1996, the court may look at how much the matrimonial home and other family assets were worth in November, 1994, not November, 1996. (Remember, this law affecting matrimonial property pertains to legal marriages only, not common-law relationships.)

2. Topics in a separation agreement

Although there is generally no limit to the issues that can be covered in a separation agreement, the most common matters dealt with include the following:

(a) Maintenance and support between husband and wife (see chapter 4)

(b) Custody, access, and support of children (see chapter 5)

(c) Release of any interest one party may have against the estate of the other in the event of death

(d) Maintenance and payment of premiums of life insurance policy by one spouse naming the other spouse or children as beneficiaries

(e) Division of matrimonial assets that may include stocks, bonds, personal chattels, and real property such as house, cottage, or vacant land (see chapter 6)

(f) Release from further claims and agreement not to claim for further maintenance or support by way of litigation

3. What happens if one spouse fails to live up to the agreement?

Like any other agreement, if one party seeks to break it, there is going to be a hassle. But if this happens, the agreement has great strength. The maintenance provisions, if any, are a debt, enforceable in court like any other debt. They also carry great weight when it comes to seeking maintenance orders in Family Court or Supreme Court. Provisions regarding children and property made by the parties will generally be enforced by the courts if they are not contrary to public policy and are in the best interest of the children.

To simplify enforcement, it is advisable to register your separation agreement with the Provincial Court or Supreme Court. This requires sending a copy of the signed agreement to the court closest to your home. If your agreement was made before July 1, 1995, you must send consent forms as set out in Sample #4, signed by each of the parties to the agreement. As you see, it is necessary to sign the consent form before a lawyer or notary public.

The advantage of registering the separation agreement is that it makes the provisions about maintenance, custody, and access enforceable by the court just as though you actually had a court order covering those items. To illustrate the difference, suppose you have a separation agreement that requires your spouse to pay child support of $200 per month. Six months have gone by in which no payments have been made. If the agreement has not been registered, you would have to start an action for maintenance or, alternatively, sue your spouse on the basis of the separation agreement — just as though it was a contract between two unrelated parties. If you followed that course of action, you would find yourself, after going through all the legal procedure, in receipt of an order — or judgment — against your spouse in the amount of $1 200 (the amount of the arrears). Then you would have to worry about how to enforce your order. If the agreement is registered with Family Court, it is as though you already have that order and you can get right on with enforcing it (see chapter 4).

The legal value of the agreement aside, if you have taken the time to sit down and discuss how you want the separation to be conducted and what terms and provisions you want included in it, you are more likely to carry on with and abide by your agreement. The very act of entering into the

SAMPLE #4
CONSENT FORM

CONSENT
IN THE PROVINCIAL COURT OF BRITISH COLUMBIA

PFA 023
REV. 04/91

COURT FILE NUMBER

CONSENT

I, _____ Judy Jill Splitupp _____,

consent to the filing of the attached agreement in the Provincial Court of

British Columbia and to the enforcement of all the provisions contained in the

agreement for:

    a) custody of or access to a child, or

    b) maintenance of a child or a spouse.

_____
Signature

Sworn before me

at City of Wilton,   British Columbia

on   July 2nd   , 199- .

_____
A Commissioner for Taking Affidavits for British Columbia

FILE

agreement has value. And, upon any subsequent court hearing, the agreement is extremely good evidence as to what the parties originally intended.

An alternative to signing a separation agreement and having it registered with the court is to enter into a consent order. We suggest you have a lawyer or family court counsellor attached to the court assist you in the preparation of such a document. It may be possible to have this document signed by the judge as a "desk order" without the necessity of either party actually having to appear in court. The court registry can advise you of the practice in that specific court.

You're likely wondering which of these two options is the better route. Generally, a separation agreement covers a large array of issues, as you can see by Sample #3, whereas the consent order deals with just the basics — custody, access, guardianship, and support.

The courts do not view with sympathy people who change their minds, and the person seeking to overturn a term in a separation agreement or consent order that he or she signed must have a very strong and good reason for doing so. If it was appropriate at the time you agreed to it, then the obvious question is, "Why has it now ceased to become so?"

4.   How effective is a separation agreement
      when I get a divorce?

You may think it strange, but the divorce court actually has the power to disregard a written separation agreement. This is because the Divorce Act gives the court supreme jurisdiction in determining the questions of custody, access, child support, and interspousal support. However, if the separation agreement is fair and both parties have had independent legal advice, the court will give it considerable, if not conclusive, weight in deciding the issues. Otherwise, the court may merely adjudicate the issues on the basis of the evidence presented at the trial.

d. WHAT IS DESERTION?

Desertion is a withdrawal from the matrimonial relationship without just cause or excuse and with the intention of terminating the marital cohabitation. But it is really an outmoded term now as far as the law is concerned. Today, the Divorce Act makes no reference to desertion. It just looks to see whether the spouses were living separate and apart for at least one year prior to granting the divorce. It doesn't matter who left whom.

The Family Relations Act does not consider desertion either. It sets out factors to be considered in making an award of spousal support or division of matrimonial property and conduct is *not* included.

e. HOW DO I GET MY SPOUSE OUT OF THE HOUSE?

Husband and wife almost always are considered to have an equal right to live in the matrimonial home. It can, therefore, be very difficult to get one party out of the house without resorting to the courts. The test in British Columbia in determining whether an order ought to be made giving one party exclusive possession of the home is that he or she must show that the shared use of the matrimonial home is a practical impossibility and that he or she be preferred as an occupant *on a balance of convenience.*

Before you can apply for an order giving you exclusive possession of the home, you must start an action for divorce or an action under the Family Relations Act for a declaration that you and your spouse have no reasonable prospect of reconciliation. Your application for exclusive possession is then made to the Supreme Court. It is a "chambers motion," which means you don't appear and give evidence in person but rather the judge decides on the basis of sworn affidavits. This is a complex procedure and should not be attempted without the help of a lawyer.

If you fear that your spouse will cause you or the children personal injury or that he or she will damage the property, you may apply for a peace bond or a restraining order. These remedies are discussed further in sections **j.** and **k.**

If the judge is satisfied that there are reasonable grounds for your fears, he or she could order your spouse to enter into a "peace bond" for a period of time up to one year. Various terms might be attached to this, including, possibly, a term that your spouse not enter the home where you are living.

If matters have escalated to the point that your spouse has threatened you or physically assaulted you, he or she could be charged with a criminal offence. If convicted, the accused might be put on probation with a condition that he or she not enter the matrimonial premises. (See sections **k.** and **l.** following for more details.)

An alternative to the legal process is to simply put your spouse's belongings outside the house and change the locks on the doors. However, there is no law against someone breaking into his or her own house, so this method may not work at all.

If you find the situation intolerable and, for whatever reasons, cannot have your spouse ejected, your best bet may be to temporarily relocate and, if necessary, bring a court action against your spouse for sufficient support to enable you to live elsewhere. The various ways of doing this are discussed in chapter 4. Before taking such a drastic step however, you should consult with a lawyer.

Under the Family Relations Act, it's clear that the matrimonial home is a family asset and, as such, each party is usually entitled to one-half of the value of the property regardless of in whose name the house is registered. (In some cases a spouse may have a different share entitlement than one-half and you should check with a lawyer.) If your spouse agrees to sell it, you merely list the house for sale in the ordinary way. If he or she doesn't agree, it is possible to apply to the court for an order for sale.

The court may make such an order unless it means ousting the parent with custody and the children and leaving them in a financial position where it is impossible to obtain adequate alternative housing. In such situations, often the court postpones the sale until the children are older — perhaps until they have completed school.

Remember, these comments about joint ownership of the family home apply to *legal* marriages. In common-law situations, the house belongs to the person whose name is on the title unless and until the court says otherwise.

f.   THE MECHANICS OF MOVING

Ideally, the spouses should discuss the move and the division of their belongings. If that is not possible, and you decide to leave without warning, don't clean out the house! Under the Family Relations Act, spouses are entitled to an equal division of furniture and household belongings upon separation or divorce, so take approximately one-half of the total value of the belongings. If you have the children with you, make sure you have enough to accommodate their basic needs too. Taking far more than your share will only aggravate an already difficult situation, and, in time, the court might order some of it returned to your spouse. This subject is discussed in more detail in chapter 6.

When considering the matter of financing the move, there are several sources of funds to think about. Credit cards in the name of both parties can be used by either one. Likewise, either party has access to a joint bank account. In some situations it may be considered advisable for the departing party to remove funds from such an account, but do what is reasonable in the circumstances. To clean out the bank account will aggravate the situation as much as will cleaning out the house and, again, will be frowned upon by the court.

If, following the move, you are in need of financial assistance, you can apply to the Ministry of Human Resources for help. If your spouse doesn't have enough income to wholly support you and/or the children, the ministry will make up the difference. You are allowed to keep $50 ($100 if you have dependants) of the maintenance payment received each month without the amount of social assistance being reduced. Anything over that results in an equivalent reduction in the amount of social assistance. So, for example, if a wife who is on social assistance receives $200 per month maintenance from her husband, her "welfare cheque" would be reduced by $150 — or by $100 if she has children.

g. CAN MY SPOUSE BOTHER ME WHEREVER I LIVE?

If you have moved out of the matrimonial home and established your own separate residence, your spouse has no right to be there, and there are legal grounds for having him or her ejected. In this case, the police should assist although they may not wish to interfere in such a domestic situation. Should they refuse to do so, you are entitled to physically eject your spouse, using no more force than is necessary.

h. WHAT SHOULD I DO IF MY SPOUSE ASSAULTS ME?

In some cases, the separation may be a violent one. If your spouse beats you or threatens your life or health, you should immediately telephone the police.

If you have suffered any injuries, even of a minor nature, you should see your family doctor or submit to examination in the emergency ward of a hospital. You should also have a friend or relative take photographs of the injuries, as these may be used as evidence against your spouse if court proceedings are started.

Finally, your spouse may be charged for assault, threatening, or both. (This is discussed further in the next few pages.)

i. WHAT THE POLICE WILL (AND WON'T) DO

The basic duty of a police officer is to prevent breaches of the criminal law. This includes assaults, public disturbances, and breaking and entering. The police will come to quell violence and little else unless other laws are being broken. Where a hostile situation exists and there is a danger of violence, they will frequently urge one party or the other to leave for the night, or they will deliver a severe dressing down in the hopes of calming the situation.

If you find it necessary to telephone the police, tell them the problem, the offence being committed or feared, and ask them to come. Be brief, to the point, and businesslike. Do not attempt to involve them in the argument or expect them to take sides. They will be interested only in seeing that the law is obeyed and will not regard it as their function to give you or anybody else advice about rights. They will want only the facts.

j. THREATS, ASSAULTS, AND PEACE BONDS

We've outlined below some of the legislation available to protect a complainant.

1. Assault

One person may not physically assault another and is liable to court prosecution if he or she is so unwise as to do so.

Assault

265.(1) A person commits an assault when

(a) without the consent of another person, he applies force intentionally to that other person, directly or indirectly;

(b) he attempts or threatens, by an act or a gesture, to apply force to another person, if he has, or causes that other person to believe upon reasonable grounds that he has, present ability to effect his purpose;

. . .

Remember that the merest shove may be enough to constitute assault. The result of a conviction for a first offence would usually be a suspended sentence and a period of probation for a number of months. A term of the probation order could be that the accused have no contact with you, directly or indirectly. If your spouse breaches this term, he or she may be brought back to court and sentenced further or may be charged with breach of probation. The sentence for this would likely be a short period in custody. A deterrent perhaps equal to the threat of jail is the stigma of a criminal record.

A popular misconception is that the assault victim does the charging. This is not so; the *state* makes the charge. Therefore, the victim does not have an automatic right to withdraw the charge if he or she subsequently decides not to proceed. The state (in the person of the prosecutor) may insist that the case go ahead.

2. Peace bond

The procedure is different if you want a peace bond under section 810(1) of the Criminal Code, which reads as follows:

Any person who fears that another person will cause personal injury to him or his spouse or child or will damage his property may lay an information before a justice.

The spouse requesting the peace bond should contact the police and have them investigate the concerns. The spouse must then attend in person to the provincial court and swear an information before a justice of the peace (J.P.). The J.P. will want to see a copy of the police investigation notes before this is done. From that point on, the procedure is the same as for an assault charge. The defendant will be summonsed to court and the judge will decide if there are reasonable grounds for the informant (the spouse who swore the information) to fear personal injury or property damage. If so, the defendant may be required to enter into a recognizance to keep the peace and be of good behavior for up to a year. If the defendant doesn't abide by this, he or she is guilty of a breach of recognizance and can be fined or sent to jail. *AFTER THAT SCARE + PRIOR I WAS NOT A THREAT TO ANYONE, JUST WANTED TO BE HEAR*

Whether the matter is an assault charge or an application for a peace bond, it will be handled in court by the prosecutor (a lawyer retained by the government), so it is not necessary for the victim to hire his or her own lawyer.

3. Intimidation

A third option in the Criminal Code is a charge of intimidation (section 423). One spouse may not intimidate another in an attempt to force him or her to do or not do something. This often arises when parties are separated and one continually comes around to harass the other.

We have never seen this section used in a matrimonial matter, likely because of the provisions of the Family Relations Act, outlined below, that address the same concerns.

4. Order restraining harassment

Section 37 of the Family Relations Act states that on application, a court may —

> make an order restraining any person from molesting, annoying, harassing, communicating, or attempting to communicate with the applicant or a child in the lawful custody of the applicant or both the applicant and a child.

5. Order prohibiting interference

Section 38 of the Family Relations Act is what is commonly known as a restraining order. It is restricted to cases where the person seeking the restraint has custody of a child, whether by court order or separation agreement. The court can order that a person not enter the premises where the child is and that he or she not contact the child or the person who has custody or access to the child.

If you wish to use either of these last two remedies, contact either a lawyer or Family Court counsellor who can assist you in making an application through Family Court.

In September, 1995, B.C. set up a protection order registry in order to provide police with a central data base of all current restraining orders and peace bonds that contain protective conditions. As soon as such orders have been signed by the judge, the court registry faxes them to the protection order registry. You may wish to double check, just to ensure this is done.

The protection order registry also contains a victim notification system to ensure protected persons are notified when an offender is due to be released from custody.

k. CAN I WITHDRAW A CHARGE AGAINST MY SPOUSE?

As discussed earlier, the state, not you, lays the charge, and so it is up to the prosecutor whether or not to withdraw the charge. You should be very reluctant to even make this request.

A charge should never be withdrawn merely because the person charged is attempting to frighten you. Should you give in to this form of pressure, you will never again be able to exert any control over that person as he or she will then know that any charges can ultimately be stopped. This will reinforce the impression that he or she can always win over you and you will end up in a worse position than before.

In addition, should you withdraw a charge, you will have caused the court staff and police considerable work and effort for nothing, and you will lose your credibility with them. Consequently, should you find in a week or month's time that you again have to lay a charge, you will have difficulty getting help from them because you have already "cried wolf."

1. LEAVE ME ALONE!

Often, once the parties have separated, or even while they are still living together, one harasses the other. One phones at all hours of the night and day, continually drives around the other's house, accosts him or her in the street or at work, continually comes into the home and generally makes life miserable. This type of situation can become extremely aggravating and often there is nothing that can be done about it, mainly because of the difficulties of compiling hard evidence that it is actually occurring.

If this happens to you, one obvious answer is for you to take up residence under an assumed name and to get an unlisted phone number. Calling the police can be effective to remove an obnoxious person from the front door, but usually nothing can be done about deep breathing exercises over the telephone at 3:00 a.m.

When one of the spouses is living separately from the other and is maintaining his or her own residence, the other spouse has no right whatsoever because of the marital status to demand entrance into that residence.

Some husbands feel that even though they are living apart from their wives they can have sexual intercourse with them whenever they desire; this is erroneous. The man may be charged with a sexual assault. In these situations the police should be called at the first opportunity.

As mentioned, in these cases one party can obtain a form of restraining order or injunction against the other ordering him or her to cease the harassment. Problems like these should be discussed with a lawyer or Family Court counsellor to see what solutions are available.

Evidence is always necessary in any of these matters, and you might be well advised to invest in a camera (preferably a Polaroid) and start taking photographs of your spouse when he or she appears on the scene. Also, accurate notes should be kept of the time, date, and place of these episodes of harassment so that when the matter eventually ends up in court a very accurate record can be given by the complaining party.

If your spouse knows that you are taking these careful and detailed steps with the obvious intention of court proceedings, he or she will often stop. Of course, if you are facing someone with a distorted mind, this type of tactic will not be a deterrent but will nevertheless be very useful when it comes time to give evidence in court.

3
DIVORCE AND ANNULMENT

When a marriage has broken down, usually a couple eventually wishes to dissolve their marital relationship. The marriage can be dissolved only if one or the other spouse has grounds for divorce or nullity.

a. WHEN CAN I USE THE BRITISH COLUMBIA COURTS TO GET A DIVORCE?

To obtain a divorce in British Columbia, the following conditions must be met as of the date the proceedings for divorce are started:

(a) Either the husband or the wife has had his or her usual place of residence in British Columbia for a period of 12 months before the divorce proceedings were started;

(b) No proceedings have been started in any other province.

b. HOW LONG DOES A DIVORCE TAKE?

An uncomplicated divorce proceeding, that is, a divorce in which all outstanding matters with regard to children, maintenance, and property have been resolved or do not arise, usually takes approximately three months to complete in Vancouver. In areas outside Vancouver, the time may vary.

It is no longer necessary to have a court hearing for the granting of a divorce. You may simply file documents with the court registry and the court will process your divorce, provided it is uncontested.

The court will issue a divorce order, which may contain other orders (e.g., the support and custody of children), provided there is something in writing indicating that the husband and wife consent to those orders being made. Thirty-one days after the pronouncement of the divorce order, the court will issue a certificate of divorce (upon request only), which means that the divorce is final. The husband and wife may not remarry during the 31-day waiting period. This period allows the parties to reopen the proceedings or appeal the order, and gives them a final opportunity to investigate the prospect of reconciliation. It is unusual to have a reconciliation at this stage, however. After the certificate of divorce has been issued by the court, the parties may each marry someone else.

In cases in which the court feels there are special circumstances, it may make the divorce final at a time earlier than the 31st day after the judgment is rendered, provided that both the husband and the wife agree and undertake not to appeal the divorce order or to abandon any appeal from the divorce order. The court may fix the time when the divorce will take effect.

An uncontested divorce is one in which the husband and the wife have agreed on all outstanding matters between them, and there is nothing to fight over. Usually the divorce itself is not contested, but the husband and wife may not agree on who is to have custody of the children, how much access the non-custodial parent is to have to the children, or how much money the non-custodial parent is to pay for the maintenance of the other spouse and/or the children. In addition, the writ of summons and statement of claim may include a claim under the Family Relations Act for a division of family assets. The husband and the wife may not agree on what those assets are and how they should be divided. If any of these issues are not agreed upon, then the divorce becomes contested. The petitioning spouse (the plaintiff) has the writ of summons and statement of claim served on the other spouse (the defendant), and the defendant files a document called a statement of defence or statement of defence and counterclaim to the writ of summons and statement of claim. A statement of defence or statement of defence and counterclaim sets out the areas of concern to the defendant and in this manner the court is advised that the divorce is contested and a trial date must be set. The length of time it takes to obtain a trial in a contested divorce varies from place to place; however, it would probably be approximately one year.

When a divorce is uncontested, the plaintiff has the defendant served with the writ of summons and statement of claim, but the defendant does not file a statement of defence or statement of defence and counterclaim. The plaintiff files an affidavit giving the evidence on which the divorce is based. The affidavit must show that reasonable arrangements have been made for the support of any children of the marriage. If the court is not satisfied that such arrangements have been made for the children of the marriage, it will not allow the divorce to proceed. The consent of the husband and wife to those arrangements is not necessarily sufficient to alleviate the court's concern about the children. Sufficient financial information must be filed so that the court can determine if the amount being paid for the support of the children is sufficient.

c. SUMMARY OF GROUNDS FOR DIVORCE

Under the Divorce Act, which applies to all provinces including British Columbia, there is now only one ground for divorce: breakdown of a marriage. Breakdown of marriage can be established in one of three ways:

(a) If the husband and wife have lived separate and apart for at least one year immediately before the divorce is to be granted and if they were living separate and apart at the commencement of the divorce proceedings

56

(b) If the spouse against whom the divorce proceeding is brought has committed adultery

(c) If the spouse against whom the divorce is brought has treated the other spouse with physical or mental cruelty

1. Living separate and apart

To obtain a divorce on the ground of marriage breakdown based on living separate and apart for at least one year, the spouses must be living separate and apart at the time the divorce proceeding is started. Usually in this case the husband and wife reside in separate residences. However, it sometimes happens that the husband and wife continue to live in the same home, but live entirely separate lives. To establish this, it may be shown that they do not cook for each other, clean for each other, eat together, or do any other thing that indicates they are living as husband and wife. All that is required to be proven is that there has been a complete withdrawal from the marital relationship with the intent to live separate and apart. The withdrawal can be by one spouse only, provided that spouse had the intent to live separate and apart.

On the other hand, it is not sufficient to show only a physical absence from one another. For example, a spouse may be hospitalized or serving in the armed forces or be abroad for a lengthy period of time visiting relatives, in which case the intention of destroying a matrimonial relationship is not present. Nor is it sufficient to show that no sexual intercourse took place if, at the same time, the spouses maintained a common household by sharing daily activities; however, prolonged refusal to have sexual relations may constitute cruelty.

As the philosophy of the Divorce Act is to encourage reconciliation, the parties may resume cohabitation for a period or periods totalling not more than 90 days, with reconciliation as its primary purpose, without breaking the

57

one-year separation. In addition, if either the husband or the wife become incapable of forming or having an intention to continue to live separate and apart (e.g., if either spouse becomes mentally incompetent during the period of separation), and if it appears to the court that the separation would probably have continued if this spouse had not become incapable, the one-year separation period is not considered to have been interrupted.

2. Adultery

To support a divorce action based on adultery it is not necessary to show direct proof of an act of intercourse, since the court may infer adultery from circumstantial evidence combined with proof of familiarity and opportunity.

Rarely does a plaintiff charging adultery come to a court equipped with photographs or films showing sexual intercourse. Most often the evidence would be the defendant's own admission that the adultery alleged in the writ of summons and statement of claim did, in fact, take place. Alternatively, the plaintiff may call as a witness someone who can testify to something like the following:

> I saw the defendant and a woman [or man, as the case may be] enter a house at 10 p.m. I saw the bedroom light go out at 11 p.m. I marked the door and returned at 8 a.m. the following morning and ascertained that the defendant had not left the home.

An act of adultery need only occur once for it to be used as the basis for a divorce. It's important to realize that this is the case even though the parties are already separated and a formal separation agreement has been signed. Many feel that the standard clause in a separation agreement that says, in effect, "the parties are free to go their own ways and live their own lives," means they can commit adultery with impunity. Not so.

3. Cruelty

Cruelty is defined as conduct of such a nature as to render intolerable the continued cohabitation of the spouses. It may consist of physical abuse or mental torment. The definition allows for a wide scope of complaints but the conduct complained of must be of a grave and weighty nature. One act of cruelty is not sufficient; the conduct must have been continuous. Mere incompatibility is not legal cruelty.

The test of cruelty is a subjective one in that the court is primarily concerned with the effect the conduct has on the plaintiff. The husband who beats his wife or children illustrates a clear example of physical cruelty, but cruelty is not restricted to physical abuse; mental cruelty is just as valid a basis for divorce.

Where physical cruelty is relied on, the evidence must be clear and convincing to a court. It is, therefore, useful if a witness can testify that the spouse suffered a black eye, broken bones, or other physical injuries. If you are in this situation, it is always best to have a doctor examine and treat these injuries so that his or her report can be available at the trial. Evidence of immediate complaint of the incident to friends or relatives may also help establish physical cruelty.

On the other hand, if it can be shown that the conduct of one spouse has caused the other to suffer mentally or emotionally, or both, the court will usually accept such conduct as grounds for divorce. Some examples are wilful refusal to communicate over a long period of time, continual and entire nights away from home without cause or excuse, refusal to have sexual relations, continuous harsh and undue criticism, or denial of natural love and affection. In most instances involving mental cruelty, the wronged party consults a psychiatrist, marriage counsellor, or family doctor, or discusses the predicament with relatives or friends whose reports or testimony have a great influence on the court's decision to grant a divorce judgment.

d. BARS TO DIVORCE

Even when there is sufficient evidence to establish grounds for divorce, the court may, in some circumstances, refuse to grant a divorce judgment. There are four bars to divorce that have been incorporated into the Divorce Act.

1. Condonation

Condonation involves a resumption of cohabitation with the intention of _forgiving_ the guilty spouse for his or her offensive conduct. It does not include, however, a continuation or resumption of cohabitation during any single period of less than 90 days or multiple periods totaling less than 90 days where such cohabitation is continued or resumed with reconciliation as the primary purpose.

2. Connivance

Connivance is an attempt by the plaintiff to encourage or persuade his or her spouse to commit a matrimonial offence in order to provide grounds for divorce. _BeS told Sluces & should find another woman._

3. Collusion

Collusion is a more serious matter in that the court is obliged to dismiss the writ of summons and statement of claim if it finds that the conduct of either party is collusive. This does not mean that the parties cannot have entered into a separation agreement. Collusion means _any_ action on your part to lie to the court or make up evidence so that you can get a divorce. In other words, your grounds must be legitimate, and when you go to court to testify on them, you must be telling the truth.

Both condonation and connivance are discretionary matters in that the court still has the power to grant a divorce if it feels it is in the public interest to do so, despite one of the spouses being guilty of this conduct. Condonation and connivance are bars to a divorce only when the divorce is based on adultery or cruelty. They have no application to a divorce based on one-year separation.

4. Lack of support for children

The court may also refuse to grant a divorce if reasonable arrangements have not been made for the support of the children of the marriage and will allow the divorce to proceed only once those arrangements have been made.

e. ADDITIONAL REMEDIES

In conjunction with the divorce action, you may also claim for custody and support of the children and maintenance for yourself. These issues are more fully dealt with in chapters 4 and 5. The advantage of having these issues dealt with by the judge hearing the divorce application is that any orders he or she makes have legal effect throughout Canada, not only in British Columbia. By means of a simple procedure, such an order may be registered in any province and be enforced as if it had been made in that province.

f. CAN I GET AN ANNULMENT?

This is a frequently asked question and, in most cases, the answer is no. An annulment means that the marriage has ceased to exist or has never existed at all in law. This is more than an academic consideration because of the tough jurisdictional problems that arise depending under which heading you fall. You should see a lawyer about it.

One valid ground for annulment is the lack of capacity to form a valid marriage. This may arise through a prior marriage, absence of consent to the marriage, mental incapacity that makes one of the parties unable to understand the nature of the marriage ceremony, forbidden blood relationship, or just being too young. Each of these is a ground for annulment. Most of the cases in which a marriage is void arise because a prior marriage exists, and most of these are the result of bigamy.

Lack of consent may occur as a result of duress, fear, or fraud. But the ground for annulment that is currently in the news is the basic mistake or no real intention to get married. This has happened in cases where immigrants have married Canadians merely to get into the country. Some courts have held that as long as the parties understood the nature of the marriage (no matter what the reason for the marriage was), there can be no annulment. Such arrangements may be considered acts of dishonesty and the court may refuse to help.

Usually, in these cases the marriage has never been consummated, and you might think that you would be able to get an annulment or, after one year, a divorce. However, the courts have often refused to grant either an annulment or a divorce in these circumstances.

As annulment is a very complex area, a lawyer should be consulted. The best thing, however, is not to enter into a marriage of convenience at all.

Sexual impotence sufficient to obtain an annulment is the incurable inability or incapacity of one of the parties to have normal sexual intercourse with the other, and it must exist at the time of solemnization of the marriage. An annulment is not granted because the parties *don't* have sexual relations, but rather because they *can't*.

g. CHOOSING HOW TO PROCEED

Once you decide to proceed with divorce, you are then faced with the decision of whether or not to use a lawyer. The average uncontested divorce costs will vary depending on the lawyer you choose. The range seems to be $300 to $600 plus disbursements (the lawyer's out-of-pocket expenses) which average about $190. You may, however, choose to proceed with the divorce on your own without a lawyer.

Remember, though, that considerable complications can arise and to do a divorce yourself takes time and effort which can be saved by using a lawyer. Using a competent lawyer also avoids the possibility of pitfalls and errors that may cost you grief and heartache in the future. For instance, you may have property rights or rights concerning your children that you do not realize. Many of these rights are terminated upon a divorce. Moreover, if your grounds are shaky, you will be more certain of the outcome if you choose a competent lawyer. If you cannot afford to pay for a divorce, you should try to obtain legal aid.

If your situation is simple and uncontested, you can certainly do it yourself by using the *Divorce Guide for British Columbia* and package of forms also published by Self-Counsel Press. The *Divorce Guide* sets out step by step what you must do to accomplish your task. Read the book and then decide what you wish to do.

If you decide to use a lawyer, you should be very careful to get a quote beforehand and arrange your finances accordingly. Most lawyers will allow you to pay a small retainer and make monthly deposits on that retainer so that, by the time the divorce is completed, your retainer has been built up to the full amount of the divorce fee. If one lawyer won't accept such terms, certainly the next one you talk to will, so give it a try. In some cases, too, you will be able to recover some of your costs from your spouse. Discuss this with your lawyer.

If there is more than a divorce involved or if your spouse is going to argue about maintenance, property, children, or in any way contest something, you may expect the fee to be much higher than that quoted above. In fact, the fee is likely to be so high that you and your spouse had best very seriously consider whether or not you want to fight it out in court. Discuss this with your lawyer and attempt to be very reasonable in your offers of settlement with your spouse as it is very much in your best interest to avoid a courtroom dispute.

h. PROCEDURE FOR AN UNCONTESTED DIVORCE

If you are using a lawyer, the initial step involves meeting with him or her. Make sure the lawyer is experienced in family matters (see chapter 7). The lawyer will question you on all the issues required for completion of the writ of summons and statement of claim. From the information gathered, he or she will prepare the writ of summons and statement of claim, have the action filed in the appropriate court, and then deliver copies of these documents to a process server who will then serve copies on the defendant.

If the defendant is served within British Columbia, he or she has seven days in which to file and deliver an appearance to the plaintiff. The time limit is as follows if he or she is served in the following locations:

- Another Canadian province — 21 days

- United States — 28 days

- Any other jurisdiction — 42 days

After the filing of the appearance, the defendant must file a statement of defence or statement of defence and counterclaim within 14 days of the last day to file an appearance. The statement of defence or statement of defence and counterclaim is a document outlining the points in the statement of claim that are contested. If the requisite time period has expired and no statement of defence or statement of defence and counterclaim has been filed, your lawyer may process the necessary documents to obtain the divorce order. The lawyer then files the following documents:

(a) Praecipe

(b) Applicant's affidavit

(c) Registrar's certificate of pleadings

(d) Affidavit of service of writ of summons and state-ment of claim

(e) Child support fact sheet (if there are children in-volved)

(f) Proof that no statement of defence or statement of defence and counterclaim has been filed

(g) Divorce order

The affidavit is your evidence on the divorce and must be sworn before a lawyer. If your divorce is based on adultery or cruelty, other evidence may be necessary. The court will require, for example, for an uncontested divorce based on adultery, an affidavit and interrogatories from the defendant admitting the adultery. There may be medical evidence required for an uncontested divorce based on cruelty. These pieces of evidence will be presented to the court by your lawyer when the rest of the documentation is submitted. After the court has had time to peruse the application for the divorce, provided it is prepared to grant the divorce, the divorce order is made. Thirty-one days later a certificate of divorce, which is a final formalization of the divorce, is issued, upon the filing of a praecipe requesting it. However, a final certificate of divorce is not issued if the defendant launches an appeal.

You cannot remarry until the final certificate of divorce is issued, so don't set a wedding date exactly 31 days from the day your divorce order is pronounced. You won't get it that quickly!

i. WHAT TO DO WHEN SERVED WITH A WRIT OF SUMMONS AND STATEMENT OF CLAIM

These two documents together initiate a divorce proceeding (see Sample #5). When the process server hands you a copy of each of these documents, you may be asked to produce some form of identification such as a driver's licence or birth certificate. You should comply with these requests as they do not, in any way, amount to an admission of liability. By proving your identity, you are merely confirming that the right person has been served with the documents. (The usual practice in British Columbia is for the plaintiff to provide the process server with a photograph of the defendant. This gives further confirmation that the person served is, in fact, the defendant.)

A statement of defence is delivered if you wish to dispute any claims that are made against you in the statement of claim. If you wish to assert any affirmative claims against your spouse, you may also serve and file a counterclaim, which can be contained within the same document as the statement of defence. Such claims may include a divorce itself, based on any grounds that may be available to you, custody of or support for your children, or maintenance for yourself. The same time limits apply for filing and serving the appearance and statement of defence to a counterclaim as to a statement of claim.

If you fail to take any steps within the time period, you may well lose the privilege of contesting the divorce, or, in fact, of knowing when the divorce hearing takes place. Unless you are certain that you do not wish to have these privileges, you should take steps to retain a lawyer as soon as possible after you receive these documents, and, in any event, prior to the expiration of the time period.

j. CAN WE SUE FOR DIVORCE TOGETHER?

Under the Divorce Act, the husband and wife can jointly claim a divorce, but only on the basis of one-year separation and only if nothing is asked for but the divorce. If one of the parties wishes custody or maintenance, a joint writ of summons and statement of claim is not permitted unless those orders are consented to by the other spouse. Once the writ of summons and statement of claim are filed, they need not be served. You should ensure that you have independent legal advice prior to entering into a joint writ of summons and statement of claim, just as you would prior to commencing a statement of claim or filing an appearance. They are a very important legal documents and you may have rights you are unaware of and that should be claimed in a writ of summons and statement of claim.

k. WHAT NAME CAN A WIFE USE?

When a woman marries, she is entitled to continue to use her maiden name or, at her option, may legally use her husband's name. Even if she adopts her husband's name, she cannot legally be prevented from reverting to her maiden name at any time. (This has evolved from the principle that a person may use whatever name he or she chooses, as long as its use is not calculated to deceive or inflict pecuniary loss.)

Practically, however, it is usually difficult for a wife to convince appropriate authorities (e.g., passport office, motor vehicle licence bureau) to change her official documents to her maiden name without either a court order or a final divorce judgment.

After a divorce, a woman may revert to her maiden name, a right she has had all through her marriage. However, even if she has sole legal custody over the children, she cannot legally change their names to her maiden name without her husband's consent, although this consent can be waived by a judge of the Supreme Court.

The practical answer for a woman who does not have the money to hire a lawyer to make the application to the judge but who is considering reverting to her maiden name and knows that her husband will not consent to a change in their children's name is to simply allow the children to use her maiden name and instruct the teachers to call them by that name. When the children are 19 years of age, they can apply independently to formalize their name changes.

Be aware, however, that this procedure can have unhappy ramifications if the father does not agree. He may make application to the court to restrain the children from using the mother's name or, if there are other problems, even apply for custody in the face of the attempted name change.

SAMPLE #5
WRIT OF SUMMONS AND STATEMENT OF CLAIM

No.: _____ D56789 _____

Registry:_____ Vancouver _____

IN THE SUPREME COURT OF BRITISH COLUMBIA

BETWEEN

JOAN QUE PUBLIC   PLAINTIFF,

AND

JOHN QUE PUBLIC   DEFENDANT

WRIT OF SUMMONS —
FAMILY LAW PROCEEDING

(Name and address of each plaintiff)

> Joan Que Public
> 123 Alimony Road
> Vancouver, BC Z1P 1Y1

(Name and address of each defendant)

> John Que Public
> 123 Divorce Lane
> Vancouver, BC Z1P 1Y1

ELIZABETH THE SECOND, by the Grace of God, of the United Kingdom, Canada, and Her other Realms and Territories; Queen; Head of the Commonwealth; Defender of the Faith.

To the defendant: John Que Public
                        123 Divorce Lane
                        Vancouver, BC Z1P 1Y1

TAKE NOTICE that this action has been commenced against you by the plaintiff for the claims set out in this writ.

IF YOU INTEND TO DEFEND this action, or if you have a set-off or counterclaim which you wish to have taken into account at the trial, YOU MUST:

(a) GIVE NOTICE of your intention by filing a form entitled "Appearance" in the above regis-try of this Court, at the address shown below, within the time for appearance provided for

SAMPLE #5 — Continued

below and YOU MUST ALSO DELIVER a copy of the appearance to the plaintiff's address for delivery, which is set out in this writ; and

(b) if a statement of claim is provided with this writ of summons or is later served on or delivered to you, FILE a statement of defence in the above registry of this court within the time for defence provided for below and DELIVER a copy of the statement of defence to the plaintiff's address for delivery.

YOU OR YOUR SOLICITOR may file the appearance and the statement of defence. You may obtain a form of appearance at the registry.

JUDGMENT MAY BE TAKEN AGAINST YOU IF:

(a) YOU FAIL to file the appearance within the time for appearance provided for below, or

(b) YOU FAIL to file the statement of defence within the time for defence provided for below.

TIME FOR APPEARANCE

If this writ is served on a person in British Columbia, the time for appearance by that person is 7 days from the service (not including the day of the service).

If this writ is served on a person outside British Columbia, the time for appearance of that person after service shall be 21 days in the case of a person residing anywhere within Canada, 28 days in the case of a person residing in the United States of America, and 42 days in the case of a person residing elsewhere.

[Or, if the time for appearance has been set by order of the court, within that time.]

TIME FOR DEFENCE

A statement of defence must be filed and delivered to the plaintiff within 14 days after the later of:

(a) the time that the statement of claim is served on you (whether this writ of summons or otherwise) or is delivered to you in accordance with the Rules of Court, and

(b) the end of the time for appearance provided for above.

[Or, if the time for defence has been set by order of the court, within that time.]

1) The address of the registry is:

> 800 Smithe Street
> Vancouver, BC   V62 2E1

2) The plaintiff's address for delivery is:

SCP-DIVBC-SOLE(1-2)98

70

SAMPLE #5 — Continued

123 Alimony Road

Vancouver, BC   Z1P 0G0

Phone number: (604) 555-0553

Fax number for delivery is (if any):

PLAINTIFF'S CLAIM FOR RELIEF

The plaintiff claims from the defendant the following relief (*mark boxes*):

[X] Divorce

[ ] Nullity

[ ] Judicial separation

[ ] Guardianship of child(ren)

[ ] Custody of child(ren)

[ ] Access to child(ren)

[ ] Maintenance or support of plaintiff

[ ] Maintenance or support of child(ren)

[ ] Division of family assets

[ ] Other relief (specify) _____

[ ] Costs

DATED this __15th__ day of _____June_____ 199_.

_Joan Q Public_____

Plaintiff

No.: D56789

Registry: Vancouver

IN THE SUPREME COURT OF BRITISH COLUMBIA

BETWEEN

Joan Que Public

PLAINTIFF,

AND

John Que Public

DEFENDANT

STATEMENT OF CLAIM —
FAMILY LAW PROCEEDING

The plaintiff must complete Parts A, B, C, and D of the statement of claim, leaving out those paragraphs that are not relevant and making changes and additions if necessary. The plaintiff must only complete Parts E to I if a claim is made appropriate to those parts.

If a paragraph is not completed, the remaining paragraphs must not be renumbered. If a paragraph is added, it must be given a decimal subnumber (such as 7.1, 7.2) or be continued numerically after paragraph 36.

PART A: PARTICULARS OF PARTIES

1. The plaintiff is Joan Que Public of 123 Alimony Road, Vancouver BC Z1P 0G0.
2. The plaintiff was born on January 10, 1960.
3. The defendant is John Que Public.
4. The defendant was born on September 12, 1958.
5. The plaintiff has ordinarily been resident in British Columbia since January 10, 1960.
6. The defendant has ordinarily been resident in British Columbia since July 1, 1965.
7. (Insert name and address of any other party who is joined in the action.)

SCP-DIVBC-SOLE(1-4)98

SAMPLE #5 — Continued

PART B: RELATIONSHIP OF PARTIES

8. The plaintiff and defendant were married on _____ at _____.
   (date)   (city, province)

9. ~~The plaintiff and defendant are spouses as defined by the *Family Relations Act* (give particulars if necessary to establish the status of the plaintiff and defendant as spouses).~~

10. ~~The plaintiff and defendant commenced cohabitation on~~ _____

11. The plaintiff and defendant ceased to cohabit on _____ July 30, 199-- _____.

12. ~~The plaintiff and defendant were divorced from each other by an order made on~~ _____
    _____.

PART C: CHILDREN

13. (a) ~~The children of the marriage as defined by the *Divorce Act* (Canada) are:~~

Name	Birth date	Person with whom child resides

   OR

   (b) ~~The parties are parents as defined by the *Family Relations Act* and the children of the parties are:~~

Name	Birth date	Person with whom child resides

   OR

   (c) There are no children of the marriage as defined by the *Divorce Act* (Canada).

   OR

   (d) ~~The parties are not the parents of any children as defined by the *Family Relations Act*.~~

SAMPLE #5 — Continued

PART D: OTHER PROCEEDINGS AND AGREEMENTS

14. (a) ~~The particulars and status of any other proceeding or agreement between the parties with respect to a separation between the parties, or to the support or maintenance of a party, or with respect to the division of property of the parties, are as follows (set out particulars and status):~~

OR

(b) There has been no other proceeding or agreement between the parties with respect to a separation between the parties, or to the support or maintenance of a party or of a child of a party, or with respect to the division of property of the parties.

PART E: DIVORCE

[Complete this part if the plaintiff seeks an order of divorce from the defendant or the husband and wife jointly seek an order of divorce from each other.]

15. There has been a breakdown in the marriage as defined by the *Divorce Act* (Canada) the particulars of which are as follows *(refer to specific sections of the* Divorce Act *(Canada))*:

    Pursuant to section 8(2)(a), I was living separate and apart from the defendant spouse at the commencement of this family law proceeding, and I have lived separate and apart from the defendant spouse since July 30, 199-.

16. (a) The surname of the wife immediately before marriage was _____.

    (b) The surname of the wife at birth was _____.

17. (a) The surname of the husband immediately before marriage was _____.

    (b) The surname of the husband at birth was _____.

18. The marital status of the wife at the time of marriage was _____.

19. The marital status of the husband at the time of marriage was _____.

20. There is no possibility of reconciliation.

21. There has been no collusion in relation to this proceeding. There has been no condonation of any act relied on as a ground for divorce.

22. (a) A certificate of the marriage has been filed.

    OR

    (b) ~~A certificate of registration of the marriage has been filed.~~

SCP-DIVBC-SOLE(1-6)98

74

OR

(c) ~~It is impossible to obtain a certificate of the marriage or a certificate of the registration of the marriage because *(set out reasons)*:~~

OR

(d) ~~A certificate of the marriage or a certificate of registration of the marriage will be filed before this action is set down for trial or an application is made for an order of divorce *(set out the reasons for not filing a certificate at this time)*.~~

PART F: CUSTODY, GUARDIANSHIP AND ACCESS

[Complete this part if an order in relation to the custody of, guardianship of, or access to children is sought.]

23. The children for whom an order of custody, guardianship, or access is sought are *(set out names)*:

24. (a) The children in respect of whom such claim is made have been habitually resident in British Columbia since _____.

    (date)

    OR

    (b) The grounds of jurisdiction under section 44 of the *Family Relations Act* are *(set out particulars)*:

25. The plaintiff seeks such orders under:

    (a) the *Divorce Act* (Canada),

    (b) the *Family Relations Act*, or

    (c) both.

26. The particulars of the past, present, and proposed care of the children are as follows *(set out particulars)*:

SCP-DIVBC-SOLE(1-7)98

SAMPLE #5 — Continued

PART G: SUPPORT OR MAINTENANCE
[Complete this part if the plaintiff seeks an order for support or maintenance.]

27. The plaintiff seeks an order for spousal support or maintenance under:

    (a) the *Divorce Act* (Canada),

    (b) the *Family Relations Act*, or

    (c) both.

28. The plaintiff seeks an order for child support or maintenance under:

    (a) the *Divorce Act* (Canada),

    (b) the *Family Relations Act*, or

    (c) both.

29. (a) The financial position of the plaintiff and of the children in care of the plaintiff is set out in one or more of an income statement, an expense statement, and a property statement, and the documents in which that financial position is set out:

        (i) will be served with this document.

        OR

        (ii) will be served after service of this document.

    OR

    (b) The financial position of the plaintiff and of the children in care of the plaintiff is as follows *(set out particulars)*:

30. (a) The plaintiff will require that the defendant set out the financial position of the defendant in one or more of the following:

        (i) an income statement

        (ii) an expense statement

        (iii) a property statement

    OR

    (b) The financial position of the defendant is as follows *(set out particulars)*:

SAMPLE #5 — Continued

PART H: PROPERTY

[Complete this part if the plaintiff seeks an order in respect of family assets.]

31. (a) The plaintiff seeks an order for equal division of family assets.

OR

   (b) The plaintiff seeks a reapportionment of family assets on the following grounds *(set out particulars)*:

32. (a) The assets owned by each of the parties are set out in a property statement that:

   (i)   will be served with this document.

   OR

   (ii) will be served after service of this document.

OR

   (b) The assets owned by each of the parties are *(set out particulars)*:

33. The legal description of land in which the plaintiff claims an interest is *(set out legal description)*:

PART I: OTHER RELIEF

[Complete this part if the plaintiff seeks other relief.]

34. The plaintiff seeks a change of name under the *Name Act* on the granting of a divorce order *(set out particulars)*:

35. The plaintiff seeks the following relief under the *Family Relations Act (set out any other orders sought under the* Family Relations Act, *the sections of the act under which the orders are sought, and the particulars)*:

SCP-DIVBC-SOLE(1-9)98

SAMPLE #5 — Continued

36. The plaintiff seeks the following additional relief *(set out particulars)*:

SUMMARY OF RELIEF SOUGHT
(Set out the relief claimed by reference to each part of the statement of claim and any claim for costs.)

PLACE OF TRIAL

The place of trial will be _____.

Dated this _____ day of _____, 199_____.

Jean Q Public

Signature of plaintiff

4

MAINTENANCE AND SUPPORT BETWEEN HUSBAND AND WIFE

a. SUPPORT GENERALLY

Historically, the law required a husband to maintain his wife. But times have changed and the conditions that gave rise to this no longer exist. It is not uncommon now for a wife to support the family or contribute substantially to the family income. Under the Divorce Act, and under the Family Relations Act, a husband can now seek support from his wife.

There are three sources of authority for one spouse seeking support from the other. The first is the simple law of contract — a separation agreement. If husband and wife agree on an amount of support and write it into the agreement, it is as enforceable as any other contract. Payments not made remain owed, and one can take the other to court to recover the debt.

The second source of authority is the power given to the court under the Divorce Act to award maintenance on a divorce. This, of course, applies only to a formal marriage situation and the application should be made at the time of the divorce.

The third source of authority is found under part 7 of the Family Relations Act.

b. PRIOR TO DIVORCE

1. Your claim for support

If a couple have separated amicably and agree on how much money should be paid for support, they can include a term to that effect in a written separation agreement or consent order (see chapter 2). Frequently, however, couples cannot agree. In many cases, one feels the other is entitled to nothing. You may not be able to obtain a divorce or may not wish one, but you still have the right to apply to the courts for support.

Under part 7 of the Family Relations Act, a spouse can apply for support for his or herself. "Spouse" includes persons who were married to each other or persons who lived together in a marriage-like relationship for a period of two years (including same sex relationships). Persons who lived together but were not married must bring their application for support within one year after they ceased to live together. In determining liability to pay support, the act outlines several criteria to consider:

(a) The role of each spouse in the family

(b) An <u>express or implied agreement</u> between the spouses that one has the responsibility to support and maintain the other *[handwritten: No agreement at all]*

(c) Custodial obligations respecting a child

(d) The ability and capacity of and the reasonable efforts made by either or both spouses to support themselves

(e) Economic circumstances

Except as provided above, the act requires a spouse to be self-sufficient.

2. How much will you receive?

In determining the amount of support, the court considers the assets and means of each of you and any benefit or loss

80

of benefit under a pension plan or annuity. Your capacity to provide for your own support is taken into account. You cannot simply sit at home for no reason at all, refuse to work, and expect to get support from your spouse.

Your spouse's capacity is also considered. Age and physical and mental health of both of you are taken into account. If you have lived together for a relatively short time, it is not likely that one has acquired a financial dependence on the other and, therefore, the amount of support may be little or none at all.

In determining how much support should be paid, the court looks at the accustomed standard of living of both of you. If there is enough money available, the court tries to insure that the dependent spouse can continue to lead a style of life as close as possible to the style that had been enjoyed prior to the separation.

The court also looks at the means available for the dependent spouse to become financially independent and the costs involved. If, for example, you haven't worked for a considerable length of time, you may have to take some kind of retraining, whether it be to brush up on your skills or to learn about the latest developments in your career. However, if it is desirable for you to stay home and take care of a young child, the court may feel that you should not retrain at this time and that you are not in a position to be earning income.

If it is a second marriage, one or the other of you may have an obligation to support a child or spouse from a former marriage. This factor may affect the amount that is available to provide for the new spouse, and the court will take this into account.

You may have married while in university. Your spouse might have pursued his or her studies in law, engineering, or medicine while you were out working. You may have quit school and given up your ability to engage in a meaningful career in order to maintain the financial viability of the family during those difficult times. In these circumstances, the court may frequently give you a higher periodic payment or even a lump sum to compensate you for these efforts.

3. What entitles you to support?

As previously stated, the way you have treated each other is disregarded in establishing an obligation to provide support. Before the passage of the Family Relations Act, a wife could only obtain support from her husband if she had "grounds" — if she could prove he had committed adultery, had treated her with cruelty, had deserted her, or had failed to provide reasonable support and maintenance for her.

To prove these grounds, the wife usually had to air all her dirty laundry in public. The husband could then defend the proceeding by showing that the wife had committed adultery or cruelty or had deserted him.

Happily, it is no longer necessary to go into all these details of day-to-day life in a marriage in order to get support. The only criterion is *need*. If you need support, the court, after examining all the circumstances mentioned here, will give you a support award against your spouse.

4. Where to apply

An application for support under the Family Relations Act can be brought either in the Provincial Court or in the Supreme Court. Both courts require financial disclosure but the Provincial Court, unlike the Supreme Court, lacks a procedure for a pre-trial investigation. This means that searching questions about the financial material provided has to wait until the parties are actually in the courtroom. For this reason, if either party's finances are particularly complex, the Supreme Court may be the preferable forum. The procedure in that court is more complicated and you would be wise to retain a lawyer. Likewise, if you wish an order concerning real property, the application must be brought to the Supreme Court — the Provincial Court has no jurisdiction to deal with property matters.

If you feel the Provincial Court is appropriate to deal with your situation, you should contact the court in your area to inquire about making an application. Once the application for support form is completed, the court issues a summons requiring your spouse to appear in court on the date and at the time and place stated on the summons.

The summons, together with a copy of your application and any accompanying documents, must be served on the respondent. Service may be effected by simply mailing the documents. This is fine *if* the respondent appears. If he or she doesn't, however, the judge will likely not be satisfied that the documents were actually received and will no doubt adjourn the matter with a direction that there be *personal* service. This can be done by a peace officer or any adult *other than the applicant.* That individual must then swear an affidavit of service showing the date on which the summons and other documents were given to the respondent.

Either before or at the time of the first court appearance, each party must file his or her financial information, including three copies of:

(a) a completed financial statement (see Sample #6)

(b) the three most recent income tax returns

(c) the most recent assessment notice from the B.C. Assessment Authority for any property that the party owns in whole or in part, and

(d) either —

    (i) the three most recent pay slips from the party's employer, or

    (ii) if the party is not employed, recent proof of the source and amount of income (for example, if the party is unemployed and is

SAMPLE #6
FINANCIAL STATEMENT

FINANCIAL STATEMENT

In the Provincial Court of British Columbia
Under the Family Relations Act

Court File Number

Court Location

PFA 122
Rev 2 93
Form 3

Case name
as it appears on the
application.

In the case between:
name

And:
name

Filed by:
name

Your current address
for service.

ADDRESS

PROVINCE

CITY

POSTAL CODE

PHONE

MONTHLY INCOME

My salary is paid: ☐ weekly ☐ biweekly ☐ monthly

Net Monthly Salary (see Step 1 on instruction sheet)	$
Commissions	$
Unemployment Insurance	$
Pension	$
Investments	$
Rentals	$
Business Income	$
Child Tax Benefit	$
Maintenance (if any) Due $ ____ Received $	
Workers' Compensation	$
Monthly Income of any other adult living with me	$
Income of Children (if any)	$
Other	$
Subtotal	$
Income Assistance	$
A. Income Total	$

MONTHLY EXPENSES

	Total	Children's Share
Rent	$	$
Mortgage	$	$
Property Taxes	$	$
Utilities (heat and light)	$	$
Phone	$	$
Cablevision	$	$
Home Repair & Furnishings	$	$
House/Tenant Insurance	$	$
Life Insurance	$	$
Food	$	$
Restaurant Meals	$	$
Sundries & Personal Grooming	$	$
Clothing	$	$
Laundry & Dry Cleaning	$	$
Motor Vehicle (lease or loan)	$	$
(licence, insurance, fuel & service)	$	$
Transportation (public)	$	$
Medical & Dental	$	$
Newspapers & Subscriptions	$	$
Entertainment	$	$
Alcohol & Tobacco	$	$
Gifts	$	$
Church & Charities	$	$
Maintenance Payments	$	$
Child Care & Babysitting	$	$
School Expenses	$	$
Children's Activities & Lessons	$	$
(list) ____	$	$
	$	$
Child Allowance	$	$
Other (list) ____	$	$
	$	$
B. Expenses Total	$	$ Children's Share $

If you need more space for any item on this Financial Statement, attach an extra sheet and sign it.

A. Income Total	minus	$
B. Expenses Total		$
Subtotal	minus	$
C. Debt Payment Total from page 2		$
Balance		$

84

SAMPLE #6 — Continued

MONTHLY DEBT PAYMENTS			VALUE OF ASSETS	
Credit Card	$		**Real Estate Equity**	$
Balance Owing $ _____		/MO.	Market Value $ _____	
Date of last Payment _____			Mortgage Balance $ _____	
Reason for borrowing _____			**Automobile Equity**	$
			Make and Year _____	
			Market Value $ _____	
Bank or Finance Company	$		Loan Balance $ _____	
(do not include amount owing on mortgage)		/MO.		
Balance Owing $ _____			**Other Property**	$
Date of Borrowing _____				
Date of last Payment _____			**Bank or Other Account (include RRSP's)**	$
Reason for borrowing _____				
Department Store	$		**Stocks and Bonds**	$
Balance Owing $ _____		/MO.		
Date of last Payment _____			**Life Insurance**	$
Reason for borrowing _____				
			Money owing to you	$
Other (Attach list if necessary)	$		Name of Debtor _____	
Balance Owing $ _____		/MO.	**Other** _____	$
Date of Borrowing _____				
Date of last Payment _____				
Reason for borrowing _____			(Attach list if necessary)	
C. Debt Payment Total	$	/MO.	**Asset Value Total**	$

I _____ name

of _____ address

swear that

1. I am the ☐ respondent ☐ applicant in this matter,

2. I have made a complete disclosure of my present financial situation in this financial statement, and

3. all the information in this financial statement is true.

Sworn before me
on _____ 19

at _____ British Columbia

_____
A Commissioner for Taking Affidavits for British Columbia

_____
Signature

Reminder:
Have you included 3 copies of each of the following?
* this financial statement
* your 3 most recent income tax returns
* the most recent assessment notice from the B.C. Assessment Authority for any property you own in whole or in part and
* either: - your 3 most recent pay slips from your employer, or
  - if you are not employed, recent proof of the source and amount of your income
    (e.g. your 3 most recent Unemployment Insurance benefit statements, if you are receiving benefits under the *Unemployment Insurance Act*).

The other party is required to file a financial statement before or on the day of your first court appearance. You are entitled to a copy of that financial statement.

receiving benefits under the Employment Insurance Act, the three most recent E.I. benefit statements)

If a party fails to comply with this rule, the court may order an amount up to $5,000 for the benefit of the spouse, parent, or child on whose behalf the request was made.

5. Powers of the court

Under the Family Relations Act, the courts can order the following types of support:

(a) A periodic payment (i.e., a sum of money on a monthly or yearly basis)

(b) A lump sum payment either to be paid or held in trust under whatever terms and conditions the court orders

(c) That property be charged with payment under the order

An order for support can be retroactive to the date the application in the proceeding was served on the respondent. It can also be changed by the court at any time if there has been a change in the needs, means, capacities, and/or economic circumstances of one or both of the parties. This necessitates further application to the court and usually a lawyer should be consulted.

An order for support can be made under the Family Relations Act for "spouses" who have lived together for two years and can include same-sex couples provided the application is commenced within one year of separation.

If you have a written separation agreement in which you have agreed not to sue for support, the court may feel itself bound by the agreement, unless the provisions for support set out in the agreement are unconscionable.

At the same time that you seek support, you can claim support for the children and apply to have the court determine the division of property. Only the Supreme Court can deal with the property issue so if there is any argument about property, probably your claim for support should also be made at the Supreme Court. Otherwise you will have two different courts dealing with matters that are intertwined. For example, the amount of support to be awarded to a spouse will vary depending on whether or not that spouse was awarded the matrimonial home or had to pay rent elsewhere.

If subsequently you are divorced, a support order under the Family Relations Act continues in full force and effect unless the divorce court has dealt with the question of support. In that case, the support order under the divorce will govern.

c. DIVORCE PROCEEDINGS

When your divorce comes to trial, the court can also deal with the issue of support. The Divorce Act specifies the objectives of an order for the support of a spouse. An order should —

(a) recognize any economic advantages or disadvantages to the spouses arising from the marriage or its breakdown

(b) apportion between the spouses any financial consequences arising from the care of any child of the marriage

(c) relieve any economic hardship of the spouses arising from the breakdown of the marriage

(d) as much as is practicable, promote the economic self-sufficiency of each spouse within a reasonable period of time

The Divorce Act, like the Family Relations Act, is clear that the court is not to take into consideration any misconduct of a spouse in relation to the marriage. Further, the comments made earlier regarding the effect of a separation agreement and the possibility of varying a support order under the Family Relations Act apply equally to orders under the Divorce Act.

d. INTERIM SUPPORT

A support action or divorce proceeding may take a year or longer to reach trial. Often, you cannot wait until the final disposition of the trial; you need funds to maintain yourself during this time. Simultaneously with the beginning of the litigation, you can make a summary application for what is known as "interim support."

On this type of application, the court examines your need and expenses as well as your spouse's ability to pay and awards an interim sum to enable you to live modestly pending the trial.

e. IF YOUR SPOUSE DOESN'T PAY, HOW CAN YOU ENFORCE PAYMENT?

The Family Maintenance Enforcement Act assists in the enforcement of an order for maintenance, basically by taking all the "hassle" out of your hands. The "creditor" (the spouse entitled to receive maintenance) may register the order for support with a provincial government body called the Family Maintenance Enforcement Program. The "debtor" (the spouse required to pay support) would then be notified to send the maintenance payments to the program to be forwarded to the creditor. The program then monitors the situation to ensure payments are kept up to date.

The director of the program has wide access to information about the debtor that assists in enforcing payment. The director has the right to demand from any person or public body, including the Crown, information regarding the debtor's place of employment, the location of assets, and the sources of income. If a payment is missed, the director can require the debtor to file a statement of finances. If the debtor fails to do so within the prescribed time, he or she may be ordered to pay up to $5 000 to the creditor spouse and may also face imprisonment of up to 30 days.

If a spouse is in arrears, the director can attach or garnishee money that is due to the debtor. Normally, this involves ordering the debtor's employer to send a portion of his or her salary directly to the creditor. A recent amendment to the Family Maintenance Enforcement Act means that as of November 1, 1998, payers in default of maintenance orders, when $3 000 or more in arrears, may not have their driver's licences issued or renewed. The defaulting spouse can also be summonsed to court to "show cause" as to why he or she is in arrears. If the judge is satisfied that the debtor is able to pay the arrears, the debtor may be ordered to pay the money by a particular date or pay monthly instalments over and above the regular maintenance payment. If these payments aren't made, the court may order a jail sentence of up to 30 days for each payment missed. Spending time in jail does *not* cancel the money owing.

Another remedy available is to obtain a warrant of execution from the provincial court that will allow the sheriff to seize the debtor's furnishings, car, or other eligible assets.

An order for maintenance may be filed in the Land Title Office and would prevent your spouse from dealing in any way with property registered in his or her name. This puts you in a position of strength. For example, if your spouse wished to sell the property, you could agree to withdraw the order provided that the existing arrears were paid and some other security substituted to ensure future payments. If your spouse did not wish to sell but was behind in maintenance payments, you could apply to the court to force the sale in order to satisfy your judgment.

These remedies are available to the creditor whether or not he or she chooses to use the Family Maintenance Enforcement Program, but the program does have access to information and counsel available to pursue the debtor. If you have further questions about this program, you may call 660-3281 if you live in the Greater Vancouver area or 1-800-663-9666 if you live elsewhere in the province.

f. WHAT IF MY SPOUSE LIVES OUT OF THE PROVINCE?

The Family Relations Act contains provisions that allow the court to award maintenance or enforce an existing order for maintenance even when your spouse does not live in British Columbia. All the provinces plus many American states and other foreign countries have "reciprocal legislation" that allows maintenance orders made in one jurisdiction to be confirmed and enforced in another. The following jurisdictions have reciprocal agreements with British Columbia:

(a) All of the provinces and territories of Canada

(b) These states of the United States:

California	New Hampshire
Colorado	New Mexico
Connecticut	New York
Idaho	North Dakota
Kansas	Ohio
Maine	Oregon
Michigan	Pennsylvania
Minnesota	Vermont
Montana	Virginia
Nebraska	Washington
Nevada	Wisconsin

(c) In the Caribbean:
Island of Barbados and its dependencies

(d) In Africa:
Republic of South Africa
South Rhodesia (Zimbabwe)

(e) In Europe:

Austria	Gibraltar
United Kingdom	Isle of Man
Bailiwick of Guernsey	Norway
Germany	States of Jersey

(f) In the South Pacific:

Australian Capital Territory	South Australia
Fiji	Tasmania
Northern Territory of Australia	Victoria
Queensland	Western Australia
Territory of Papua and New Guinea (including Cook Island)	New Zealand
	New South Wales

(g) In Asia:

Hong Kong
Singapore

To apply for maintenance, you may contact the Provincial Court (family division) directly. Arrangements are then made for you to testify in court as to your financial situation and anything you know about your spouse's. The judge, on the basis of your evidence alone, makes what is called a provisional order for maintenance. A transcript of your evidence plus the provisional order is then forwarded to the jurisdiction where your spouse is residing. He or she will be summonsed to the court closest to his or her place of residence. After hearing the evidence regarding your spouse's financial situation and reading the transcript of your evidence that you gave in the British Columbia court, the judge will either confirm the provisional order or vary it.

If you already have a final maintenance order — either made under the Family Relations Act or the Divorce Act — and your spouse has fallen into arrears, the reciprocal legislation allows the court in the area where your spouse lives to enforce the order in the same manner as if he or she were living in British Columbia. There is no point to such an application if you cannot say exactly where your spouse is living. In that case, you may need to employ the services of a skip-tracer.

5

CHILDREN

a. THE CUSTODY OF CHILDREN GENERALLY

It is over the custody of children that the most bitter family disputes rage, and the children are caught in the middle.

Parents embroiled in such disputes should do everything possible not to draw the children into the fray and in particular not to use them as pawns in the game of matrimonial chess. The fight should take place out of the presence of the children; when they are present each parent should honor the other. The children, too, have certain rights, and one of these rights is to have the opportunity to have a relationship with both parents.

Until the court says otherwise, parents have equal rights to the custody of children. As a result, it is often tempting for one parent to take the matter of custody into his or her own hands and physically snatch the children away from the parent with actual custody. Except in very severe circumstances, this is not usually in the best interest of the children and it seldom solves any problems.

The proper way to resolve a dispute over custody is either to reach an agreement or to apply to the proper court.

1. Jurisdiction of the courts

Generally, in order for a court to exercise jurisdiction over the children, the children must be physically within that jurisdiction, and for this reason, prior to the court granting custody to one parent or the other, it is important to see that the children are not removed from the province.

In cases in which the removal of children is threatened out of malice or in an attempt to avoid a court disposition, the courts will grant an order to the effect that the children not leave the province. Should you disobey this order, you would be in contempt of court and subject to fine or imprisonment. Of course, once a custody order is made, it is permissible to take the children out of the province unless the court has ordered otherwise.

When custody matters are before the courts, the judge disregards the feelings and rights of both parents and looks solely to the interest of the child. What is in the best interest of the child is the paramount issue. This takes precedence over any "rights" of the natural parents. Suppose, for example, that a child had been placed with a grandmother or family friend and lived with that person for several years. Then the parents decided to retrieve custody. The court might well order that the child remain where he or she is in preference to the parents if that seemed to be in the child's best interest.

The "best interest test" is also applied in determining custody of an "illegitimate" child. In the past, when a child was born out of wedlock, the mother used to have the absolute right to control the custody of the child, and the father, in law, had no rights. Gradually, the father, under the law, acquired the right to obtain custody if the mother was unfit. Now the courts have shifted their focus to the child and will award custody in accordance with his or her best interest. Neither parent stands on a better footing than the other.

A mother who commits adultery does *not* disentitle herself to custody. The court does not assume an unfaithful wife constitutes an unfit mother unless such conduct affects the well-being of the child. Again, the welfare of the child is the only interest.

2. Discrimination against fathers

Many fathers have been known to complain that custody is one area in which the law discriminates against men in favor of women. To some extent this was true, particularly with regard to infants. The courts generally followed the principle that a child of "tender years" was better off with the mother. As roles in society have changed, however, so have the legal principles. In many couples, the woman really isn't in any better position than her spouse to take on the full parenting responsibility.

Statistically, in by far the majority of cases, the mother has custody. However, this is usually a situation reached by agreement between the parties when they separate and it acknowledges that in their particular relationship the mother did play the primary parenting role. However, looking only at the cases where custody has been determined by the court, fathers have an equal chance of success.

3. Changing the custody award

With the matter of custody of children, the situation is never a closed book. It may always be brought back before the courts for further review. As a result, if one parent has the custody of the children and for some reason the situation is not working out well, the other parent may return to court and seek custody. This may occur years after the matter of custody was originally "settled." The courts would simply look again to what is in the best interest of the children.

4. Joint custody

The ultimate in civil relations between spouses — and certainly tremendous for the children *when it works* — is to do away with the whole notion of "ownership" ("*I* have custody — the kids are *mine*") and agree to share custody. This necessitates both parents *agreeing* to such an arrangement; the court rarely orders it unless both want it that way. And the parents must be able to communicate with each other so that there is consistency for the children regardless of which parent they are with at a particular time.

The mechanics of joint custody vary. If the parents reside in the same area, the children may spend a few months with mom, then a few months with dad, the close proximity allowing them to continue at the same school with the same set of neighborhood friends. Or the children may remain in the same house while the parents take turns living there with them. Or the parties may acknowledge that one parent is the "parent in residence" but the other parent plays a far fuller role than merely visiting the children every other weekend. If it works, great. More and more couples seem to be making this type of arrangement, again reflecting the more active parenting role that fathers are now playing.

b. HOW TO GET CUSTODY

1. By agreement

When you enter into a separation agreement, the matter of custody of children can be covered in the agreement. The agreement in Sample #3 includes sample clauses for this purpose.

The courts always reserve the right to review the matter of custody and support and, should the spouse without custody under the agreement decide to challenge the agreement, he or she can bring it before the courts very quickly. However, that spouse would be faced with the difficulty of convincing a judge that, once having decided to give them up, he or she should now have the children. The courts step in where the best interest of the children seem to dictate that this be done.

A separation agreement is a very useful document for the spouses because it not only sets out the voluntary arrangement but has evidentiary value as to the fitness and propriety of the parent who is to have the children. The fact that it can be challenged in court should not discourage you from entering into a separation agreement if initial agreement is possible.

2. By court application

(a) Family Relations Act

The act allows an application to be made either to the Supreme Court or to Provincial Court — either independently or joined with a claim for other relief such as maintenance.

As stated, the principle followed in determining custody is the best interest of the child. The act sets out certain criteria to be considered in making this determination:

(a) The health and emotional well-being of the child including any special needs for care and treatment

(b) Where appropriate, the views of the child

(c) The love, affection, and similar ties that exist between the child and other persons

(d) Education and training for the child

(e) The capacity of each person to whom guardianship, custody, or access rights and duties may be granted to exercise these rights and duties adequately

(b) Divorce Act

A claim for custody is commonly part of the divorce action and either husband or wife can initiate the action. Divorce hearings come under the jurisdiction of the Supreme Court and, using the power of this court, the judge can award custody even though the divorce application is unsuccessful (see chapter 3 for an explanation of divorce procedure).

c. RIGHTS OF ACCESS

Rights of access refer to visiting rights awarded a parent when the other parent has custody of the children. The occasions and frequency of access are usually arrived at by agreement between the spouses. Times are arranged that are mutually convenient and beneficial to the children.

As a matter of practice, rights of access are almost always granted because the courts feel it is a *right* of a child, and in his or her best interest, to have a continuing relationship with both parents. The exception would be if it could be shown that the visits have a detrimental effect on the child, that there is a real danger of physical or emotional harm, or that a parent has deserted the child by not communicating over a long period of time.

"Reasonable access" should be worked out between the parties. Failing this, the courts will impose a schedule which usually means that the person without custody would be entitled to access on weekends and/or during certain holiday periods — especially the summer holidays.

If the parents are at each other's throats, any contact between them, at least at the beginning of the separation, is bitter and temptation is great to use the children for one or the other's advantage. Fortunately, over time, as emotions change and understanding grows, the situation usually improves. If it doesn't, the non-custodial parent may find it virtually impossible to enforce the access order. If the parent with custody is flagrantly refusing to allow the child to visit, that parent may be found in contempt of court or found guilty of an offence under the Family Relations Act and penalized. More common, however, and much harder to deal with, is the more subtle custodial parent who brainwashes the child either deliberately or unconsciously, so that the child doesn't want to visit. Technically, the non-custodial parent could enforce the access order by having the child picked up bodily by the police and delivered to his or her place of residence — but it's not likely to be an enjoyable visit! There are some extreme cases where, regrettably, it's in the child's best interest that there be no access so the child isn't subjected to the constant conflict. One can only hope that some time down the road the parent and child can pick up the pieces and form a relationship.

Note that failure to pay child support does not in itself constitute grounds to refuse access. The two matters are treated separately by the court. If the non-custodial parent obviously has the means to pay support and has refused to do so, the court may feel that this is tantamount to deserting the child and access should be denied. If, however, the parent has failed to meet his or her support obligations because of financial hard times, it's likely that the court would still encourage access to take place.

If you have an order for access and visiting rights are being refused, you may want to consult a professional who specializes in family mediation. But if mediation fails, you may turn to the courts for assistance in enforcing the order. Section 128(3) of the Family Relations Act states —

> A person who, without lawful excuse, interferes with the custody of, or access to, a child in respect of whom an order for custody or access was made or is enforceable under this act commits an offence.

Thus, you can go to the nearest provincial court and ask that your spouse be charged with an offence if access is being denied. You do not need to hire your own lawyer to take this matter to court; Crown counsel would prosecute the case just as if it were a criminal matter. If convicted, your spouse could face a term of imprisonment. In most cases, however, at least for a first offence, the court would likely impose a period of probation. The offending spouse would have the threat of jail hanging over him or her if there were any further denials of access.

This procedure is more difficult if your access order reads "reasonable access" rather than setting out specific terms, because the spouse with custody could argue that the visits he or she was allowing *were* reasonable and that you were being unreasonable for wanting more. So you may be looking at a two-part process: first, get your access order varied so the terms of visits are set specifically; then, if access continues to be a problem, consider charging your spouse with an offence.

Note: Laying charges should be a last resort. Parents who are at war with each other are not likely to serve the child's best interest.

d. ASSISTANCE IN RESOLVING THE ISSUES OF CUSTODY AND ACCESS

As mentioned, custody cases can be the worst of legal battles and the parents should be urged to avail themselves of whatever conciliation services may be available.

1. Counsellors

Family Court counsellors are attached to both the Provincial (Family) Court and the Supreme Court. They are experienced in assisting parties to resolve custody disputes. In addition, there are some well-qualified people in private practice with agencies not attached to the court, and their services may be well worth retaining. So even if legal proceedings have been started, it's not too late to avoid the courtroom. The court will often order that a custody report be prepared by someone such as the conciliation counsellor or social worker. If the report is well done, it may be abundantly clear where the child should be.

2. Family advocates

In some cases, the Attorney General's office may appoint a family advocate to represent the child's best interest in a custody case. A family advocate is basically the child's lawyer and has the advantage of objectivity — not having to follow instructions from one or the other of the parents. After meeting with the child and speaking with people who have had an opportunity to observe him or her, such as the school teacher or family doctor, the picture may be clear.

The family advocate can then meet with both parties and their respective counsel and advise what position he or she will be taking on behalf of the child and why. And again, even at this late stage, the courtroom confrontation may be avoided.

If the matter is not resolved out of court, the family advocate plays an active role in the court proceedings, often calling independent witnesses to testify on behalf of the child's interest. The court is likely to place more weight on the evidence of these persons than those called by either parent. For example, the evidence of a psychiatrist retained and paid by one parent (who often has not even laid eyes on the other parent) is not going to be viewed as being as objective as the evidence of a psychiatrist retained by the family advocate who has had an opportunity to meet with and assess all the parties.

If you are involved in a situation in which you feel a child needs separate representation (either in a custody battle or a case of abuse or neglect), have your lawyer phone Victoria ((250) 356-8400) and speak to the person in charge to determine whether the government will agree to make such an appointment.

e. SHOULD I JUST TAKE MY CHILD?

As it has already been pointed out, until the court orders otherwise, both parents, married or in a common-law union, have equal rights of custody. However, it would appear that the parent with the actual or "de facto" custody is the one with the prior legal right, at least until a court orders otherwise.

What sometimes happens is that one parent, the one without the custody of the children, will, for one reason or another, decide to take custody without the benefit of a court order and merely show up on the spouse's doorstep and remove the children or fail to return the children after a visit. This is frequently termed "child snatching." However, it is a cruel and harsh step to take and it is seldom in the best interest of the children because it usually arises when one spouse or the other is attempting to use the children as a pawn in a game of "get the other."

There may be situations where such action is justified, for example, where the children are not being looked after properly. However, a court action for an order for custody should be brought first. If the children are in serious need of protection and are living in a dangerous situation, the matter should be reported to the Ministry of Children and Families, who should be asked to intervene and take the children out of the home.

Should you find yourself in a situation where the children have been snatched, you can go immediately to court using one of the methods described and seek an interim order for the return of the children and for custody.

Sometimes, the court will make an order for the return of the children without your spouse even having notice of the application. This is called an *"ex parte* order" and will generally be for a fixed period of time, usually for a week or two — just long enough to have the other parent served with the application and allow *both* parties the opportunity to speak to the matter in court. The courts are extremely reluctant to grant an order without hearing both sides of the story so these *ex parte* orders are only granted in very special circumstances, such as where one parent has "snatched" the child from the parent normally exercising custody.

f. CAN I JUST TAKE THE CHILDREN AND LEAVE THE PROVINCE OR COUNTRY?

The answer is yes, you probably can, but you should not. Why? First, your spouse would still likely obtain an order for custody and it is possible to have this order enforced in another province; and if you are ever brought before a judge — look out!

In addition, there is nothing to stop your "ex" from moving to the new province and obtaining a new order that could be enforced quite easily.

The last and the most important consideration is the effect on the children; you will have to conclude there is little to be gained from such a move.

The law in this area is very technical and complex. Generally, while the courts may make a custody order for children who have been taken from the province on the grounds that they are ordinarily resident in British Columbia, the problems of enforcing the order are considerable and expensive.

If you are concerned that the person without legal custody might take the children and run, you may apply to the court for an order restraining your spouse from removing them from the province. Breaching such an order would leave the offending spouse subject to penalty for contempt of court. Also the court in the jurisdiction to which the offending spouse goes would be more likely to refuse to deal with the matter and direct that the children be returned to British Columbia because of the existence of an order here.

To summarize, contempt of the courts of this province would be likely to show the person contemptuous of all courts and thus render his or her reception in the court of another jurisdiction less favorable.

When dealing with orders made in another jurisdiction we are in an area of law called "conflicts of law" or sometimes "private international law," and it is a very specialized and complicated area. The advice of a lawyer must be sought immediately.

g. CUSTODY WHEN A PARENT DIES

If the parents were living together or were separated and had agreed to joint custody, then the child would continue in the custody of the surviving parent. If the parents were separated and the custodial parent died, the survivor would not automatically have custody. For example, if the custodial parent had a will designating someone else as guardian, that person would assume custody. The surviving parent would certainly have an opportunity to challenge this in court, and the decision would be based, not on his or her rights as a parent, but rather on what appeared to be in the child's best interest.

h. MUST MY SPOUSE SUPPORT OUR CHILDREN?

1. Who pays child support?

When dealing with children, the court must always be concerned that they are adequately maintained. The obligation to maintain children financially falls on both parents. This obligation continues even if the spouse with custody remarries. For example, as often happens, the wife remarries and the "ex" feels he can stop payments to the children. This is not so *unless* the new husband formally adopts the children. Often, the new husband voluntarily assumes the expenses of upbringing, but there remains a legal obligation on the natural father to continue to pay support.

Even if you are not the natural parent of the child and have not adopted the child, you might still find yourself in a position where you have to support him or her. Under the Family Relations Act, if you and the child's parent were legally married and you contributed to the support of the child for at least a year, you could be liable to pay ongoing support after your marriage terminated. If you and the child's parent were not married but lived together for at least two years and you contributed to the child's support for at least one year, again a claim for child support could be made against you. The action for support would have to be brought within a year after the date you last contributed to the child's support. This same rule applies to same sex couples.

Under the Divorce Act, you must support a child if you stand in place of a parent to the child. That means that you have acted as a parent toward the child and supported him or her in the past.

If the court has awarded custody of the children to the mother, the father is, in most cases, required to pay support. Even where custody is awarded to the father, the mother may be required to pay child support if she is financially able to do so.

2. How are child support payments calculated?

The children are entitled to enjoy the same standard of living as they would have enjoyed if the parties had not separated. As far as possible, they should be saved from the hardship caused by a marital breakdown.

The amount of child support is determined by reference to the child support guidelines. These guidelines came into effect on May 1, 1997, for child support ordered as part of a divorce order. On April 14, 1998, they were also proclaimed in force for the Family Relations Act.

Before this change in the legislation, the courts would determine the amount of child support by looking at the financial circumstances of *both* parents. The needs of the parties and their respective circumstances were also considered. A great deal of discretion was left to the trial judge. Now there are tables for awarding child support which are province specific and take into account only the income of the paying parent regardless of the income of the custodial parent. The schedules are graduated for the number of children being supported. For example, a paying parent with a $30 000 income with one child will pay $268, but if there are two children, the amount will not double, but will be $448. The guidelines are intended to reduce conflict between parents and to establish fairer, more consistent child support payments throughout the country.

The B.C. guidelines are shown in the Appendix. To use the tables, move down the left hand column until you reach the annual income of the payer. Then move across the page to the column dealing with the number of children involved.

Generally, the annual income figure will be determined using the same sources of income as are set out under the heading "Total Income" in the T1 general form that is issued by Revenue Canada. You would use the B.C. guidelines if the person who is required to pay child support lived in B.C. The figures differ slightly from province to province.

3. Can the guideline amount be adjusted?

Child support guidelines need to have a degree of flexibility, because not all children or families are alike. They are designed to strike a balance between the need for more consistent and predictable awards and the need to ensure that awards are equitable in individual situations. Support awards can be adjusted in two ways to recognize individual family circumstances.

(a) Special child-related expenses

While the guidelines reflect average expenditures on children, some kinds of expenses for children do not lend themselves to averages. To ensure that support awards are equitable when there are extraordinary expenses for a child, four categories of special child-related expenses can be added to the guideline amount if they are reasonable and necessary in light of the needs of the children and the means of the parents:

(a) Child care expenses

(b) Medical and health-related expenses

(c) Educational expenses

(d) Extraordinary expenses for extracurricular activities that allow a child to pursue a special interest or talent or attend a specialized program.

When appropriate, the support-paying parent's contribution to these special expenses will be added to the guideline amount.

(b) Undue hardship

A court will be able to award more or less than the guideline amount plus allowable special expenses if this total amount causes "undue hardship" to either parent or to the child. The party pleading undue hardship will usually have to show that he or she has a lower standard of living than the other party. The situations which might justify a finding of undue hardship are not limited to, but could include the following:

(a) An unusually high level of debt, reasonably incurred to support the family or earn a living

(b) Significant access expenses, such as travel or accommodation costs

(c) Obligations for the support of other children or spousal support obligations

The guidelines provide a method for adjusting the support amount in cases of split custody (when each parent has custody of one or more children of the marriage) and shared custody (when parents fully and equally share custody of the children).

The provincial government has trained child support clerks to assist parents who receive or pay child support. They will help parents seeking to change child support court orders or written agreements that were made before May 1, 1997. They will also help parents who don't already have a child support order in place and are applying for one according to the guidelines. They can also assist those seeking to change the tax treatment of existing orders and agreements. Information is available to anyone through written, telephone, or in-person inquiries. And for those who are eligible, the clerks can calculate support amounts according to the guidelines and help with tax election forms. For more information, you can call your local family justice centre or Enquiry B.C. at 1-800-663-7867.

You can get child support by proceeding in one of the following ways:

(a) Under the Family Relations Act, you can apply either to the Provincial Court or to the Supreme Court. Child support generally continues to age 19, but could cease earlier if the child marries or becomes self-supporting prior to that age. Alternatively, it can continue past age 19 if the child is unable, because of illness, disability, or other cause, to withdraw from the parent's charge or to obtain the necessities of life.

(b) Under the Divorce Act, an order for child support can be incorporated into the divorce judgment. Support terminates at age 16 unless the child is still dependent for the same sorts of reasons as apply under the Family Relations Act. Continuing education is a common cause for dependency.

4. Are child support payments tax deductible?

Child support paid under an order or agreement made *before* May 1, 1997, is deductible by the payer and will have to be included in the income of the recipient for income tax purposes.

Child support paid under an order or agreement made *after* May 1, 1997, is neither deductible by the payer nor included in the income of the recipient. This is the case, too, if an order or agreement made prior to May 1, 1997, is subsequently changed (after May 1, 1997) to increase or decrease the amount of child support payable.

i. HOW CAN I ENFORCE OR CHANGE A SUPPORT ORDER?

To vary or rescind a child support order, a court must be satisfied that a change in circumstances as provided for under the child support guidelines has occurred since the making or last variation of the child support order. If the court is so satisfied, the court then applies the guidelines to determine what change in the amount should be made.

The procedure to enforce or vary a child support order is exactly the same as for a maintenance order for a spouse and is discussed in chapter 4.

j. HOW IS CHILD SUPPORT HANDLED IN SEPARATION AGREEMENTS?

If a separation agreement addresses support of the children, a lot of problems and difficulty for both spouses can be avoided. Usually, the agreement is that one spouse will pay so much per month and the other spouse will not seek more than that in court. Such an agreement is legally binding to the extent that the amount may be collected by way of civil action for debt.

However, the courts have always taken the view that a parent cannot contract away the rights of the children to support from the other parent. Thus, a clause purporting to release one parent from having to pay any child support might well be overturned by the court.

The courts will look very closely at the terms of a separation agreement when considering whether or not to allow a change in the amount of child support. The court would look to see if the amount the parties had agreed to was different than the amount would have been if they'd used the child support guidelines. If so, the court would only confirm the amount the parties had agreed to if satisfied that reasonable arrangements had been made for the support of the children.

k. "ILLEGITIMATE" CHILDREN AND CHILD SUPPORT

The Family Relations Act requires a parent to pay support for a child up to the child's 19th birthday *regardless* of whether or not the spouses are living common-law or are married. In other words, the law regarding child support is the same whether or not the child is "legitimate."

Note that in addition to child support, the mother can recover payment for expenses arising from and incidental to the following:

(a) prenatal care for herself or the child, or

(b) the birth of the child.

What if the man denies that he is the father of the child? If he is a step-father and the time limitations outlined in section **h.** of this chapter are met, it makes no difference that the child isn't "his." But if the relationship between the mother and her partner is more casual and they have not lived together for two years, then the man would have to pay support only if he was found by a judge to be the biological father. This might require hearing evidence from witnesses to support the mother's story that she and the alleged father had sexual relations about nine months before the birth of the child or that the man had referred to the child as "his."

Alternatively, blood tests of the mother, child, and alleged father may be taken and introduced as evidence to show the percentage likelihood that the man is the father. The court may order a party to submit to such a test. If that person still refuses to comply, the court may make an adverse inference from the refusal (i.e., it may infer that the person disputing paternity is the father).

l.   APART FROM CHILD SUPPORT, WHAT RESPONSIBILITIES DO PARENTS HAVE TOWARD THEIR CHILDREN?

Parents are entrusted with the care, custody, and control of children until they reach the age of majority. This is ancient law that reaches back beyond memory and has, until the last few centuries, been largely a matter of social custom. Today, there are basic rules and procedures set out in the law.

The parent/child relationship with its inherent duties and obligations supposedly continues until the age of majority (in British Columbia, age 19), but there is nothing the courts can practically do to enforce this. Whether parental control continues to age 19 is more a matter of fact, not law.

Beyond the age of 19, children are adults and on their own and the relationship in law between parents and children from that point on is essentially that of strangers, even though they may continue to have close personal relationships.

Parents must maintain, protect, and nourish their children, and failure to do so is a criminal offence. To make the task of parents easier, it has always been the law that parents may use reasonable force in keeping their children in line and this is recognized in the Criminal Code. However, excessive force or abuse of children will bring rapid and severe punishment once the matter is brought before the courts. It may even result in the children being removed from the home and placed elsewhere.

m. WHAT RESPONSIBILITIES DO CHILDREN HAVE TOWARD THEIR PARENTS?

Under the Family Relations Act, a child over the age of 19 is liable to maintain and support a parent who is dependent by reason of age, illness, infirmity, or economic circumstances. Thus, the parent may make an application for support from a child in the same manner that a spouse would apply for support from a spouse. The same procedures for enforcement of such orders are available to parents and children as are available to spouses.

n. HOW DO I ADOPT A CHILD?

There are two ways to adopt a child in British Columbia: either privately or through the Ministry of Children and Families. The law states that a child may be placed for adoption with one adult or two adults jointly, and there is no requirement that the two adults be a heterosexual couple. The only legal requirement is that each prospective adoptive parent must be a resident of B.C.

Anyone who wishes to adopt a child may apply directly to the Director of Adoption. A social worker with the Ministry of Children and Families will conduct the interviews and investigations and complete the documents required by the Adoption Act. In the case of adoptions through the ministry, a lawyer's services are not usually required.

It should be pointed out, however, that because of the increasing use of contraceptives and availability of abortions, there are now very few unwanted newborn infants. Also, social attitudes are changing toward the single parent, so many previously unwanted children are being kept by their mothers. The result is a long waiting list, particularly for healthy Caucasian infants.

Couples who adopt usually do so because, for one reason or another, they cannot have children of their own. Because of the demand for children, single people or people living common-law have less chance of adopting the children in high demand.

In the case of a private adoption, unless the person applying to adopt is a blood relative of the child in question, the Director of Adoptions will still be involved to the extent of investigating the home and reporting to the court the results of that investigation.

In 1991, the Adoption Act was amended to establish a "reunion registry." The adult adoptee can contact the registry and ask for help in contacting a birth parent or a birth sibling who was also placed for adoption. The registry will then make discreet inquiries of that party as to whether they wish contact. If the answer is yes, the registry will assist in making that happen. The same service is available should a birth parent request contact with an adult adoptee. The legislation does contain a veto power allowing a birth relative or adult adoptee to specify that he or she *not* be contacted except if a compelling medical need for contact exists.

Note that the registry deals with *adult* adoptees — the person who was adopted must be at least 19 years of age before they can be assisted.

o. WHAT ABOUT ADOPTING MY SPOUSE'S CHILDREN OR ALLOWING MY SPOUSE TO ADOPT MY CHILDREN?

A step-parent adoption is certainly possible but there are some important issues to consider. A basic consideration is finances. If you are receiving child support payments from the child's parent, be aware that he or she will no longer be required to make these payments once the adoption order is made.

Is the natural parent likely to consent to the adoption? If not, it may require a lengthy and costly court hearing to determine whether or not his or her consent should be dispensed with. If that parent has any kind of relationship at all with the child, the court is unlikely to make such an order. The court takes the position that the child has the right to know both parents and will sever that tie only in rare instances.

Often the motivation behind a step-parent adoption is a desire to terminate the non-custodial parent's right to access. However, the court may order that an access order or an access provision of a separation agreement continue if the court finds this to be in the child's best interests.

Note that if the child in question is 12 or older, that child must consent to the proposed adoption.

p. CHILDREN AND THE LAW

The children of today represent the society of tomorrow, and, to a very great extent, the quality of care and training our children receive determines the quality of our society in the years to come. For centuries the law did not really become involved with children or the family unless for some reason the family was disrupted and the children were somehow ejected out of a family situation to fend for themselves.

It is only within the last 50 years or so that the law has begun to take a more active role, but today there are statutes that give clear and ample power to the various government authorities to step into any situation for the purpose of protecting and maintaining children. The power is there, but in practice it is still only in very serious cases that these agencies will actually intervene. There is tremendous public pressure placed upon the government to stay out of the personal lives of the citizens. This means that government agencies are very reticent about walking into a family situation unless there is a very clear and pressing need to do so.

1.   A parent's legal duties toward a child

Apart from the duties set out in the Family Relations Act, discussed in the earlier chapters of this book, the Criminal Code embodies certain specific duties.

DUTY OF PERSONS TO PROVIDE NECESSARIES

...

215. (1) Every one is under a legal duty

(a) as a parent, foster parent, guardian, or head of a family, to provide necessaries of life for a child under the age of sixteen years;

(b) as a married person, to provide necessaries of life for his spouse; and

(c) to provide necessaries of life to a person under his charge if that person

> (i) is unable, by reason of detention, age, illness, insanity, or other cause, to withdraw himself from that charge, and

> (ii) is unable to provide himself with necessaries of life.

(2) Every one commits an offence who, being under a legal duty within the meaning of subsection (1), fails without lawful excuse, the proof of which lies upon him, to perform that duty, if

> (a) with respect to a duty imposed by paragraph (1)(a) or (b),

>> (i) the person to whom the duty is owed is in destitute or necessitous circumstances, or

>> (ii) the failure to perform the duty endangers the life of the person to whom the duty is owed, or causes [or is likely to cause the health of that person to be endangered permanently] or

> (b) with respect to a duty imposed by paragraph (1)(c), the failure to perform the duty endangers the life of the person to whom the duty is owed or causes or is likely to cause the health of that person to be injured permanently.

. . .

Abandoning child

218. Every one who unlawfully abandons or exposes a child who is under the age of ten years, so that its life is or is likely to be endangered or its health is or is likely to be permanently injured, is guilty of an indictable offence and is liable to imprisonment for a term not exceeding two years.

. . .

214. In this part

"abandon" or "expose" includes

115

(a) a wilful omission to take charge of a child by a person who is under a legal duty to do so, and

(b) dealing with a child in a manner that is likely to leave that child exposed to risk without protection.

Is there an offence for "contributing to delinquency"? No, is the short answer. A person can be charged, however, with interfering with a disposition imposed on a young offender if he or she assists the young offender to escape custody, or assists the young offender to breach a term of his or her probation.

2. What role does the government take?

As has been pointed out already, the Criminal Code offers a certain amount of protection to children in the sense of punishing the individuals failing to provide the necessaries of life to a child or abandoning a child. The Child, Family, and Community Service Act is designed not to punish the offender but to protect the child.

This is often required not only where a child is being abused by the parents but also where the parents are unable to care for the child; where they are dead or missing; where the child has run away from home; or in any other situation in which a child is in need.

If a social worker has reasonable grounds to believe that a child needs protection and that his or her health or safety is in immediate danger, or that no other less-disruptive measure is available which is adequate to protect the child, the worker may remove the child from the parents' care. Should this occur, the worker must present a written report to the Provincial Court within seven days. At this time, a date will be fixed for a court hearing to determine whether or not the child is in need of protection.

The parents or guardians must be given notice of this hearing and they have the right to be present, to be represented by a lawyer to speak for them, to cross-examine the witnesses, to call their own evidence, and to argue before the judge as to their feelings on what the outcome should be. If the child is 12 years or older, he or she, too, must be given notice of the hearing.

Unfortunately, given the volume of cases, there is often considerable delay before such a hearing can take place. That raises the question of where the child should be in the interim. Sometimes a short hearing must be held to determine the answer.

At the conclusion of the protection hearing, if the judge finds that the child is, in fact, in need of protection, an order may be made returning the child to the parents (but under the supervision of the social workers) or there may be an order that the child remain in care either temporarily or permanently.

We should emphasize that the power to remove a child is used only as a last resort. The social workers are committed to helping the family function as a unit where at all possible, where this doesn't compromise the safety and well-being of the child.

Very often a citizen will see mistreatment of a child and wonder what to do. The law is that every citizen (including police officers, lawyers, and doctors) must report such incidents to the Ministry of Children and Families immediately. A phone call to the local ministry office is likely your quickest way to convey your concerns. Every complaint must be investigated.

What if you're the parent someone has complained about? If the ministry contacts you, wishing to carry out an investigation, our advice is to co-operate. The social workers are concerned about the welfare of your child. If, as some-times happens, the report to their office have been false (perhaps made by the other party in a custody case in an effort to discredit you), the ministry staff will be quick to end their involvement.

q. WHAT RIGHTS DO CHILDREN HAVE BEFORE THE LAW?

We have seen that there are laws requiring that children be supported, fed, and nourished. Failing this, there are certain branches of the government that have the right to step in on behalf of children.

The rights of children to enter into contracts, to marry, and to generally deal in public affairs are severely limited by the law. We have already seen the restrictions on children marrying and the consent that they require.

In B.C., the law dealing with children entering into contracts is governed by the Infants Act. With few exceptions, a contract made by someone under 19 is unenforceable unless it's affirmed once the child reaches the age of 19.

The Infants Act also deals with a child's right to consent to medical treatment. The child can consent, without the necessity of the parent or guardian also consenting, so long as the health care provider is satisfied that the consent is informed and that the treatment is in the child's best interest.

The issue of children's rights often arise in the area of family law. All too often, there is a sense that children are part of the "bartering" that occurs when the parents decide to separate — "If I can have the kids, you can have...." We've discussed the role of the family advocate under section **d.** of this chapter. The involvement of such independent counsel can help to ensure the focus is kept on the children's best interest.

r. HOW ARE CHILDREN PROSECUTED UNDER THE CRIMINAL LAW?

In Canada, children under the age of 18 are prosecuted by procedures under the Young Offenders Act, which has tried to strike a balance between the needs of young people and the interest of society. The act contains a Declaration of

Principle stating that society must be protected from the illegal behavior of young persons and thus they are to be held responsible for their acts. Because of this, the young person is to be afforded all of the protection an adult receives in our criminal justice system.

The declaration goes on to acknowledge that in view of their level of development, however, young persons will not in all instances be held as accountable for their behavior as adults. An example of the lesser degree of accountability is reflected in the dispositions available under the act. When an offence is committed — criminal, motor vehicle, liquor, or certain others — the police carry on their investigation in much the same manner as in any other case. However, once it is determined that a young person is involved, the procedure becomes markedly different.

The police send a report to the prosecutor who reviews it to see whether a charge is proper, that is, whether the circumstances support a charge and whether there's sufficient evidence to prove it.

Once that stage is passed, the prosecutor then considers the youth who has committed the offence. If it is a person who has not been in trouble before, and if the offence is a fairly minor one, the prosecutor will likely write to the youth's parents, outline the circumstances, and leave it to them to take proper disciplinary action. If the charge is more serious, the prosecutor may refer the matter to a probation officer to carry out a pre-court inquiry. The probation officer contacts the youth and the family and recommends that —

(a) the matter proceed to court,

(b) there be no further action, or

(c) the youth be diverted (i.e., dealt with outside the formal court setting).

For this last alternative to be used, the young person must acknowledge responsibility for the offence, otherwise the case must be dealt with in court. The alternative measures suggested by the probation officer might include things such as writing an essay, restitution, community service work, or some form of counselling. There will be no formal record of a conviction. The final decision rests with the prosecutor.

If the youth already has a record, or if the charges are a serious concern in the community, no pre-court inquiry is conducted and the matter proceeds directly to court.

If there is to be court action, a summons is delivered to the parents as well as the youth, and a parent must attend court to prove the youth's age. The young person must have been over 12 and under 18 at the time the offence was committed. At the first appearance, the judge asks the young person if he or she has talked to a lawyer. Normally, there is duty counsel present to speak to the youth and advise him or her what to do at this early stage. If the youth asks the judge to appoint a lawyer for him or her, the judge *must* do so and there is no cost to the accused or his or her family. The matter is then generally adjourned several weeks to allow time for this appointment to be made and for the lawyer to learn the details of the alleged offence. On the next court date, if the youth pleads guilty, the prosecutor relates the circumstances to the judge. The judge almost always asks for a report from the probation officer before sentencing the offender. This pre-sentence report outlines the youth's background, education, home life, criminal record, and so on. With this information, the judge decides the sentence that would best benefit the child and the interest of society.

If the youth pleads not guilty, the case is adjourned for a trial, at which point the prosecutor calls evidence to prove the allegations beyond a reasonable doubt as in any adult case.

s. WHAT CAN THE YOUTH COURT DO TO A YOUTH WHO IS FOUND GUILTY?

The Young Offenders Act tries to balance the young person's needs with the public interest and emphasizes the protection of the public. There is a wide range of dispositions available:

(a) If the offence is relatively minor, the court may, if it finds that it is in the best interest of the accused and not contrary to the public interest, instead of convicting the accused, order that he or she be discharged absolutely or on conditions set out in a probation order.

(b) A fine not exceeding $1 000 may be imposed.

(c) The youth can be ordered to pay an amount to the victim of the offence as compensation for loss of or damage to property, loss of income or support, or for special damages for personal injury arising from the offence where the value can be easily determined.

(d) There can be an order that property be returned to the victim or that the youth compensate the victim by way of personal services.

(e) The young person can be required to perform community service (e.g., doing volunteer work for a community group, visiting a senior citizens' home, or perhaps cleaning up a park area). The maximum number of hours that may be assigned is 240.

(f) The young person may be detained for treatment if it appears he or she is suffering from a physical or mental illness or disorder, a psychological disorder, an emotional disturbance, a learning disability, or mental retardation.

(g) A period of probation may be imposed for up to two years.

(h) Most seriously, the youth may be detained in custody. The maximum length of the custodial sentence depends on the nature of the offence.

> (i) For first degree murder, the total sentence may be ten years (six of which may be spent in custody),
>
> (ii) For second degree murder, the total sentence may be seven years (four of which may be spent in custody),
>
> (iii) For other offences for which an adult could conceivable receive a life sentence, a young person faces a maximum custodial sentence of three years, and
>
> (iv) For all other offences, the maximum is two years.

(i) The court can impose whatever other reasonable conditions seems advisable in the best interest of the young person and the public.

If parents are having problems with their child, they may ask the judge to impose special additional terms to the probation such as curfew, not associating with certain people, or going certain places.

You should try to discuss the matter first with the probation officer, but if this is not possible then it should be suggested to the judge at the time of sentencing. When sentencing is taking place, step forward and wait until the judge recognizes you and asks you to speak; then express your concerns.

The situation is somewhat different where the offence alleged is extremely serious: murder, manslaughter, or aggravated sexual assault. If the young person was 16 or 17 at the time of the alleged offence, he or she is dealt with in adult court *unless* defence counsel succeeds in an application to have the matter moved to youth court. Conversely, if a 14- or 15-year old is charged with one of these offences, the Crown counsel can apply to have the matter moved to adult court. If the trial does take place in adult court and the young person is convicted, the sentence imposed is not necessarily what an adult would receive, but may well be longer than what the youth court could impose.

t. CAN THE YOUTH COURT BLAME PARENTS FOR THEIR CHILD'S OFFENCE?

The Young Offenders Act recognizes that parents are responsible for the care and supervision of their children but this concept does not extend to vicarious liability. Parents cannot be ordered to pay a fine, damages, or costs when a child is found guilty of an offence.

u. WHERE CAN I TURN FOR HELP CONTROLLING MY CHILD?

Sometimes, parents find themselves in the situation of having a child under 19 who is beyond their control. The solution may well require the involvement of all family members in counselling, or a mental health professional may be required if the problem stems from a mental disorder. Drug and/or alcohol abuse may be involved and, again, there are resources available to deal with the addicted child.

Our advice is to contact the Ministry of children and Families who can advise you of the various individuals or agencies available. If your problem is extreme, the Director may even step in as a temporary guardian to the child — either by way of a short-term care agreement or a court order for temporary custody.

6

PROPERTY DISPUTES

a. WHO OWNS WHAT IN A COMMON-LAW MARRIAGE?

In section **c.** below, the family assets approach in the Family Relations Act is discussed. This is the presumption that each spouse has an equal interest in property ordinarily used for a family purpose.

The property division provisions of the Family Relations Act do not apply to common-law spouses or to same-sex spouses. However, they will apply to common-law spouses if those spouses enter into an agreement that would have been a marriage agreement or separation agreement if the spouses were married to each other. It is not known as yet how this provision will be interpreted by the courts.

If property is jointly acquired and put into the names of both parties, there should be no dispute over the fact that each is entitled to a half interest. But what if the property was acquired by only one party (perhaps before the common-law relationship even began) and then either the whole or a half interest is given to the other party?

Generally, the law says that a gift between common-law spouses is permanent and irrevocable. This presumption can be rebutted by clear evidence to the contrary, but in most cases this evidence is not forthcoming because oral evidence alone is generally very weak and conflicting. The simple rule is that you are presumed to have the intention that would be the natural intention behind your act. For example, if you make an apparently outright gift to someone, you are presumed at law to have intended to make an outright gift. As you must incur a great deal of trouble and expense to rebut this presumption, be careful when making gifts to a common-law spouse.

What is much more common, and much more complicated to determine, is a situation in which the parties jointly acquire property but it is put into the name of one party alone, or a situation where one party owns property alone but the other spends untold hours working on the property and improving its value.

As the number of common-law relationships increases, so do the number of property disputes of this kind. If one spouse can persuade the court that there was a common intention that the property belong to both spouses, the court will find that the property-owning spouse actually holds a certain portion of the property "in trust" for the other and that the one party is entitled to be paid for this interest. Those cases are rare. In most instances the "common intention" can't be proved.

However, there is still a remedy open to the party who doesn't own the property. If he or she can show the court that the other has been "unjustly enriched" at his or her expense, then again the court may find the existence of a trust. For example, the common-law wife on a farm is a familiar situation. Her common-law husband owned the farm before he met her. She moved to the farm and worked diligently over many years raising animals, helping with the haying, etc. Then the relationship ended and the "husband" said "Sorry, dear, the farm is mine."

If the court hears from witnesses who knew that the husband regularly referred to the farm as "ours" and had promised his "wife" that she would be rewarded for her efforts by sharing in the farm, that common interest would be present and the husband would be found to own a portion of the farm as trustee for the wife. If this isn't the case, the court may find that the husband benefited at the wife's expense and, again, would find that he owns a portion of the farm as trustee for her.

It's a complicated and expensive matter to argue about in court, so the best advice to a common-law spouse is to get your name on the title.

b. WHAT IS THE DIFFERENCE BETWEEN OWNERSHIP AND POSSESSION OF PROPERTY?

Ownership means a right in the legal title to the property itself; possession means a right to use or occupy the property. This distinction is important because the law treats ownership disputes between husband and wife differently from possession disputes. In other words, a wife may not "own" the family home, but normally she does have a strong claim of possession. The procedure for the adjudication of either of these disputes is set out in the Family Relations Act.

c. THE FAMILY ASSETS APPROACH

The concept of family assets presumes that a family should be treated as one economic unit.

A family asset is defined in section 45(2) of the Family Relations Act as "Property owned by one or both spouses and ordinarily used by a spouse or a minor child of either spouse for a family purpose." Therefore, the family car, the bank account that is used for household purposes, the boat, the cottage, and the house are all family assets. So, too, are such items as pensions and registered retirement savings plans.

Even property used primarily for your spouse's business purposes may be classed as a family asset if it can be shown that you made a contribution to the acquisition of the property or the operation of the business; and the act makes it clear that fulfilling the role of a homemaker constitutes a contribution.

Upon separation or divorce, either spouse is entitled to go to the court and ask for an equal division of the family assets. Normally, the court distributes these assets equally. To prevent injustices in some specific cases, the court has jurisdiction to make an unequal division of family assets in certain circumstances.

If you have entered into a marriage agreement setting out the division of family assets, that will be considered. If you have lived together for only a short time, equality of economic status may result in injustice. Therefore, the court will take into account how long you lived together while married.

It will also take into account how long you have been separated. The date when the property was acquired will be of interest to the court. If one of you acquired property by gift or inheritance from some third party, that will be taken into consideration when assessing whether an equal division of the asset is fair. In addition, the court may take into account any other relevant circumstances relating to the property or how it was used or how it was maintained or acquired when assessing whether an equal division is fair. Family debts may be taken into consideration when deciding whether an equal division is fair. Only the Supreme Court of British Columbia has jurisdiction to deal with these types of issues. The Family Court has no jurisdiction.

Your spouse cannot defeat your claim by putting a piece of property in the name of a corporation. For example, if the husband owns shares in a corporation that owns the family home, his shares in the corporation form part of the family assets and they are subject to equal division.

If your spouse threatens to get rid of some of the property that has been in his or her name during the marriage in order to prevent a fair and equal division upon separation or divorce, the court may make an order restraining such disposition. The court has very wide powers of discretion in deciding what to do with family assets. It can order the re-allocation and transfer of specified property; it can order the sale of any property and the division of the proceeds; it can charge any property with any obligation imposed by its order; it can order one spouse to pay the other a sum of money in order to make a property adjustment in family assets.

Only people who are married to one another or who have been divorced less than two years can take this approach. Common-law spouses or people who have been divorced more than two years cannot avail themselves of these provisions of the Family Relations Act.

d. OWNERSHIP OF THE MATRIMONIAL HOME

1. What is joint tenancy?

Couples who purchase a home for themselves and their family often have the legal title placed in joint tenancy. Title in this form involves two important legal implications:

(a) If either spouse dies, title to the entire property legally passes "automatically" to the survivor without forming part of the estate of the deceased. This is known as the right of survivorship.

(b) If the spouses sell the property, each is entitled to receive one-half of the net proceeds of the sale because each spouse owns one-half of the house.

2. Who owns the home if legal title is in the name of one spouse only?

Under the Family Relations Act, any property that has been ordinarily used for family purposes becomes a family asset. Obviously, this includes the matrimonial home. As discussed earlier, as a family asset, the home will usually be split 50-50 between the spouses at the time of separation or divorce regardless of the spouse on title to the property. The court does have the jurisdiction to vary the equal division if it is "fair" to do so.

It is possible to "contract out" of this division if you and your spouse agree that an equal division isn't what you want. The act allows you to enter into an agreement dealing with how property is to be owned, managed, or divided. If the property is registered in the name of your spouse only and you have concerns that the property may be sold or mortgaged without your approval (or without your knowledge!), it is possible to register your agreement in the Land Title Office. This effectively stops the property in question from being dealt with in any way without your consent.

Another safeguard that is open to a non-owning spouse is filing a lien under the Land (Spouse Protection) Act. This amounts to swearing an affidavit that the property in question has been the residence of you and your spouse within the last year. The affidavit and various accompanying documents are filed in the Land Title Office and, again, this is sufficient to restrict your spouse from dealing with the property in any way without your consent.

e. POSSESSION OF THE MATRIMONIAL HOME

Each spouse is equally entitled to be in possession of the matrimonial home unless the parties themselves have reached an agreement to the contrary and embodied this in an agreement or unless the court orders otherwise. The Provincial Court cannot make such an order. You must apply to the Supreme Court for an order excluding one spouse from the premises. *ownership ?*

A dispute over possession of the property will be greatly affected by who has custody of the children. If there are no children, the court seems to look at how intolerable one spouse is making life for the other. Such an order is for temporary relief only pending determination of the rights to the property.

As previously mentioned, this determination of rights doesn't necessarily mean that the property must immediately be sold. The court may find the spouses entitled to an equal division of the new equity in the property yet postpone any sale until such time as the children are finished school, for example. So the temporary right to exclusive possession may, in fact, continue for some years. However, this is an unusual outcome.

Although each party is entitled to an equal division of the contents of the home, since they are family assets, the court may postpone such division and permit the person who occupies the home to continue to have the use of some or all of the contents. Frequently, the court decides who is responsible for repairing and maintaining the home and paying the mortgage payments, hydro payments, water payments, and all other expenses of living in a home.

f. WOMEN'S RIGHTS TO CONTRACT AND INCUR DEBTS

According to law, women are on an equal footing with men as far as their rights to borrow money and enter into contracts are concerned. However, this is of little practical value because, as a matter of practice, it may be difficult for a married woman to find an institution that will lend her money in her name alone unless she has adequate security. This business policy renders her legal right to borrow money rather useless.

The reasons evolve from history and experience. Women, according to history, are poor credit risks because they have more difficulty finding employment, tend to hold lower paying jobs, and are frequently prevented from obtaining work because of their children. Although this may not be their fault and the result may be very unjust, it is a fact of life.

It is a very difficult thing for a woman to get on her feet financially once she is separated from her husband, especially if she has children to raise. Financial institutions take all this into consideration but adequate counselling in financial matters is very difficult to get. Resources that you can turn to, however, are bankers and some lawyers.

Debts that have been incurred by the husband and co-signed by the wife are the equal responsibility of both.

However, generally when either party contracts a debt after the separation, in his or her own name, it does not affect the other.

One of the exceptions to this is an old common-law doctrine that a wife may charge her husband's credit for necessaries. Although a husband had no obligation to support his wife, he did have an obligation to supply her with the necessaries of life, and if he failed to do so, she could go to any merchant and obtain food and clothing and have the merchant bill her husband who could be compelled by the courts to pay. This was a beautiful remedy in theory, but, of course, very few merchants are happy to get involved in such disputes and again the law and the practice are widely divergent. Consequently, this right has dimmed considerably in importance and is very difficult to enforce.

Of course, if the husband and wife have joint credit cards, there is joint liability as long as those accounts remain open and neither party has cancelled them. In this case there would be joint liability with both parties being responsible for payment of the bills.

g. THEFT BETWEEN SPOUSES

It is often thought that a husband and wife cannot be charged with stealing from each other, but this is not strictly the case. Where a marriage is on the rocks, it is possible that one can be charged with stealing from the other as section 329 of the Criminal Code makes most clear.

> 329. (1) Subject to subsection (2), no husband or wife, during cohabitation, commits theft of anything that is by law the property of the other.
>
> (2) A husband or wife commits theft who, intending to desert or on deserting the other or while living apart from the other, fraudulently takes or converts anything that is by law the property of the other in a manner that, if it were done by another person, would be theft.

(3) Every one commits theft who, during cohabitation of a husband and wife, knowingly

   (a) assists either of them in dealing with anything that is by law the property of the other in a manner that would be theft if they were not married, or

   (b) receives from either of them anything that is by law the property of the other and has been obtained from the other by dealing with it in a manner that would be theft if they were not married.

This section is rarely, if ever, used because of the difficulties involved in proving the theft. However, it is possible for a charge to be laid and prosecuted by the Crown. If a spouse feels particularly vindictive, such a charge may be laid even though there is little chance of its being successful. Reason does not always prevail in these situations, and the spouse making the complaint may see some value in the nuisance factor involved in such a charge, if nothing else.

7

LAWYERS AND LEGAL AID

a. LAWYERS

1. How to choose a lawyer

There is no secret method for choosing a good lawyer — no more so than choosing a professional person in any other field such as medicine, accounting, auto mechanics, or plumbing.

Ask your friends and relatives if they can recommend anyone — or warn you away from anyone. But keep in mind that just because your brother's lawyer is good at conveyancing, it does not follow that he or she will be good in family law matters. There are so many areas of law that many lawyers concentrate on specific areas.

If you cannot get a recommendation and you live in any of the major centres in British Columbia, you have available to you a Lawyer Referral Service (listed under that heading in the phone book). If you call them and request a lawyer experienced in family law, they will make an appropriate referral. You are entitled to half an hour of consultation for $10. Past that point you are charged at the lawyer's regular rate. By that time you should be able to tell whether you would like the particular lawyer to act for you. Don't be afraid to discuss the fee; it's perfectly acceptable to shop around.

2. Be prepared

Before you see your lawyer, prepare yourself in writing. Write out your name, address, age, place of birth, children's names, and the names of all the other people involved in your problem with as much information about them, their work, and living situations as you can. Then write out a brief history of your problem, how it came about, what happened, and what you want done. The lawyer will want to know details about your financial circumstances and that of your spouse. Put some thought into it, so that when you go to see your lawyer you can hand over the sheet. In this way you will also have in your own mind a fresh, clear picture of the situation.

Do not go to see your lawyer without any idea of what you want, or of who is involved, or without all of the documents and information. You will only be told to go away and come back when you have it all together. Every minute is costing you. Don't waste time and then blame the lawyer because the bill is high. Whether your lawyer gets anything done or not, you are paying for his or her time.

3. How much will it cost?

A lawyer has nothing to sell but time. He or she has no other product. Accordingly, the fee will reflect the amount of time, whether on the telephone, in the office, or over lunch, that your case consumes. Should you call him or her at home, expect very high billings for that. Of course, if you want to keep your lawyer working for you, call him or her at home only in the most extreme emergencies. Everything that you do to save time, everything that you can do for yourself, will keep your bill down.

Frequently, lawyers are not prepared to wait to bill you until the whole case is completed. As previously stated, the case can take a long time until it is fully disposed of. As a result, lawyers will often send interim bills as the matter progresses. Feel free to discuss this with your lawyer before deciding to retain him or her.

If there is a dispute involved — with a spouse, for example, or over children or property — it may not be possible for your lawyer to pinpoint exactly how much the bill will be because it is impossible to say how much time will be involved. It will depend on how the dispute goes, what the other side does, and what difficulties arise. In that case, you should ask for an estimate based on an hourly rate.

Virtually all lawyers have been stung by clients who do not pay. The solution is to get the fee in advance (usually called a retainer). It is usually not the full fee but a good portion of it. It is held in a special account, called the trust account, and used only for items such as court fees that must be paid for on your behalf. The lawyer can use it only if he or she sends a bill to you setting out the details of the account. When you deliver the retainer, get a receipt.

Often the person seeking help has no cash. Some lawyers accept property as a retainer, and others work with little or no retainer. If you are seeking help and you have a house in joint tenancy or a spouse who would be able to afford court costs that might be awarded, it is often possible to get the lawyer to act if you turn over these proceeds at a later date. Talk to your lawyer about it.

The court may award costs to a successful party. Costs are based on a tariff and amount to a contribution to your legal fees — they usually will not cover your entire legal bill. However, it is completely up to the court as to whether costs should be awarded to either party.

b. GOVERNMENT-APPOINTED LAWYERS

The provincial government provides counsel in certain matters before the Family Court under these circumstances:

(a) If one party is being charged with a criminal offence or with an offence under the Family Relations Act (for disobeying a custody or access order, for example), Crown counsel will prosecute the case and hiring a private lawyer is not necessary.

(b) If the applicant has custody of a child and there has been violence or a "reasonable apprehension of violence," counsel will be provided until a final order is obtained.

(c) If the applicant is receiving social assistance, he or she has the option of asking the ministry to apply for maintenance or child support on his or her behalf. If the applicant chooses this way of proceeding, counsel will be provided.

(d) If an order for maintenance or child support has been made and is not being obeyed, counsel will be provided to enforce proceedings if the order has been registered with the Family Maintenance Enforcement Program.

c. LEGAL AID

The legal aid system in British Columbia, although supported by the provincial government, is not a government program with unlimited funds to assist people with legal problems. Because of the limited funds, there are restrictions on the type of matters legal aid will pursue.

There are two tests to determine eligibility. The first is a "means" test. A person is eligible if the person's monthly household income (after deductions) is at or less than the scale set out below:

Number in family	Maximum monthly net income to qualify
1	$ 941
2	$1 412
3	$1 647
4	$1 821
5	$2 008
6	$2 183
7 or more	$2 333

The second hurdle is that even if you are financially eligible, legal aid is not available for all family matters. Coverage is available for the following:

(a) If your family problem is serious, for example, if your or your children are at risk of abuse or if you may lose contact with your children

(b) If you need help to start getting maintenance or child support payments and there is no other organization that can help you

(c) If you are a respondent in a maintenance enforcement proceeding and will go to jail as a result of it

(d) If your children have been removed by the Ministry of Children and Families

Legal aid is *not* available to do the following:

(a) Change or enforce an existing maintenance or child support order

(b) Change a custody or access order, unless your children are at risk of harm and that risk has been confirmed in writing by a health care professional

To apply for legal aid, residents of the Greater Vancouver area can apply at the Family Law Clinic, 1270 – 605 Robson Street in Vancouver. In other areas, residents should apply to the legal aid clinics operated by the Legal Services Society in that area. Look in the Yellow Pages under "Lawyers;" there will be a subheading "Legal Aid — Legal Services Society."

APPENDIX
CHILD SUPPORT GUIDELINES
FOR BRITISH COLUMBIA

Income/ Revenu ($)	Monthly Award/ Palement mensuel ($) No. of Children/ Nᵇʳᵉ d'enfants				Income/ Revenu ($)	Monthly Award/ Palement mensuel ($) No. of Children/ Nᵇʳᵉ d'enfants				Income/ Revenu ($)	Monthly Award/ Palement mensuel ($) No. of Children/ Nᵇʳᵉ d'enfants				Income/ Revenu ($)	Monthly Award/ Palement mensuel ($) No. of Children/ Nᵇʳᵉ d'enfants			
	1	2	3	4		1	2	3	4		1	2	3	4		1	2	3	4
6700	0	0	0	0	12000	99	157	179	201	17300	144	257	347	394	22600	198	337	449	542
6800	0	0	0	0	12100	99	160	183	205	17400	144	258	349	398	22700	199	339	451	544
6900	2	3	3	4	12200	99	163	186	209	17500	145	259	351	401	22800	200	340	453	546
7000	5	6	7	8	12300	99	166	189	212	17600	146	261	353	405	22900	201	342	455	549
7100	7	9	10	12	12400	99	169	192	216	17700	147	262	355	409	23000	202	343	457	551
7200	10	12	14	16	12500	99	172	196	220	17800	148	264	357	412	23100	203	345	459	553
7300	12	15	17	20	12600	100	175	199	223	17900	149	265	358	416	23200	204	346	461	556
7400	15	18	21	23	12700	101	177	202	227	18000	150	267	360	420	23300	205	348	463	558
7500	18	21	24	27	12800	102	180	206	231	18100	151	268	362	423	23400	206	350	465	560
7600	20	24	28	31	12900	103	183	209	235	18200	152	270	364	427	23500	207	351	467	562
7700	23	27	31	35	13000	104	186	212	238	18300	153	271	366	431	23600	208	353	469	565
7800	26	30	34	39	13100	105	189	215	242	18400	154	273	368	434	23700	209	354	470	567
7900	28	33	38	43	13200	106	192	219	246	18500	155	274	370	438	23800	210	356	472	569
8000	31	36	41	47	13300	107	195	222	249	18600	156	276	372	442	23900	211	357	474	572
8100	33	39	45	51	13400	108	198	225	253	18700	157	277	374	446	24000	212	359	476	574
8200	36	42	48	54	13500	109	200	229	257	18800	158	279	376	449	24100	213	361	478	576
8300	39	45	52	58	13600	110	203	232	261	18900	159	280	378	453	24200	214	362	480	578
8400	41	48	55	62	13700	111	205	235	264	19000	161	282	380	457	24300	214	364	482	581
8500	44	51	59	66	13800	112	207	239	268	19100	162	283	382	460	24400	215	365	484	583
8600	47	54	62	70	13900	113	208	242	272	19200	163	285	384	464	24500	216	367	486	585
8700	49	57	66	74	14000	114	210	245	275	19300	164	286	386	467	24600	217	368	488	587
8800	52	60	69	78	14100	115	211	248	279	19400	165	288	387	469	24700	218	370	490	590
8900	54	63	72	82	14200	116	213	252	283	19500	166	290	389	471	24800	219	371	492	592
9000	57	66	76	85	14300	117	214	255	287	19600	167	291	391	473	24900	220	373	494	594
9100	60	70	79	89	14400	118	216	258	290	19700	168	293	393	476	25000	221	375	496	597
9200	62	73	83	93	14500	119	217	262	294	19800	169	294	395	478	25100	222	376	498	599
9300	65	76	86	97	14600	120	219	265	298	19900	170	296	397	480	25200	223	378	500	601
9400	68	79	90	101	14700	121	220	268	301	20000	171	297	399	483	25300	224	379	502	603
9500	70	82	93	105	14800	122	222	271	305	20100	172	299	401	485	25400	225	381	504	606
9600	73	85	97	109	14900	123	223	275	309	20200	173	300	403	487	25500	226	382	506	608
9700	75	88	100	113	15000	124	225	278	313	20300	174	302	405	489	25600	227	384	508	610
9800	78	91	104	116	15100	125	226	281	316	20400	175	303	407	492	25700	228	386	510	613
9900	81	94	107	120	15200	125	227	284	320	20500	176	305	409	494	25800	229	387	512	615
10000	83	97	111	124	15300	126	229	287	323	20600	177	306	411	496	25900	230	389	514	617
10100	86	100	114	128	15400	127	230	291	327	20700	178	308	413	498	26000	231	390	516	619
10200	89	103	117	132	15500	128	232	294	330	20800	179	309	414	501	26100	232	392	518	621
10300	91	106	121	136	15600	129	233	297	334	20900	180	311	416	503	26200	233	393	520	624
10400	94	109	124	140	15700	130	234	300	337	21000	181	312	418	505	26300	234	394	521	626
10500	96	112	128	144	15800	131	236	303	341	21100	182	314	420	508	26400	234	396	523	628
10600	97	115	131	147	15900	131	237	306	344	21200	183	315	422	510	26500	235	397	525	630
10700	97	118	135	151	16000	132	239	309	348	21300	184	317	424	512	26600	236	399	527	632
10800	97	121	138	155	16100	133	240	312	351	21400	185	318	426	514	26700	237	400	529	634
10900	97	124	142	159	16200	134	241	316	355	21500	186	320	428	517	26800	238	402	531	636
11000	97	127	145	163	16300	135	243	319	359	21600	187	321	430	519	26900	239	403	533	638
11100	97	130	149	167	16400	136	244	322	362	21700	188	323	432	521	27000	240	405	534	640
11200	98	133	152	171	16500	137	245	325	366	21800	189	325	434	524	27100	241	406	536	643
11300	98	136	156	175	16600	138	247	328	369	21900	191	326	436	526	27200	242	408	538	645
11400	98	140	159	178	16700	138	248	331	373	22000	192	328	438	528	27300	242	409	540	647
11500	98	143	162	182	16800	139	250	334	376	22100	193	329	440	530	27400	243	411	542	649
11600	98	146	166	186	16900	140	251	337	380	22200	194	331	442	532	27500	244	412	544	651
11700	98	149	169	190	17000	141	252	341	383	22300	195	332	443	535	27600	245	413	545	654
11800	98	152	173	194	17100	142	254	343	387	22400	196	334	445	537	27700	246	415	547	656
11900	98	154	176	198	17200	143	255	345	390	22500	197	335	447	540	27800	247	416	549	658

Income/Revenu ($)	Monthly Award/Paiement mensuel ($) — No. of Children/N^bre d'enfants			
	1	2	3	4
27900	248	418	551	660
28000	249	419	553	662
28100	250	421	555	664
28200	251	422	557	667
28300	251	424	558	669
28400	252	425	560	671
28500	253	427	562	673
28600	254	428	564	675
28700	255	429	566	677
28800	256	431	568	680
28900	257	432	569	682
29000	258	433	571	684
29100	259	435	573	686
29200	260	436	575	688
29300	260	438	577	690
29400	261	439	579	693
29500	262	440	581	695
29600	263	442	582	697
29700	264	443	584	699
29800	264	444	585	700
29900	265	445	587	702
30000	266	446	588	704
30100	267	447	590	705
30200	267	448	591	707
30300	268	449	593	709
30400	269	451	594	711
30500	269	452	596	712
30600	270	453	597	714
30700	271	454	598	716
30800	272	455	600	717
30900	272	456	601	719
31000	273	457	603	721
31100	274	458	604	723
31200	274	459	606	724
31300	275	460	607	726
31400	276	462	609	728
31500	276	463	610	729
31600	277	464	612	731
31700	278	465	613	733
31800	279	466	615	735
31900	279	467	616	736
32000	280	468	618	738
32100	281	469	619	740
32200	282	471	621	742
32300	282	472	622	744
32400	283	473	624	745
32500	284	474	626	747
32600	285	475	627	749
32700	285	477	629	751
32800	286	478	630	753
32900	287	479	632	755
33000	288	480	634	757
33100	288	481	635	759
33200	289	483	637	761
33300	290	484	638	762
33400	291	485	640	764
33500	292	486	642	766
33600	292	487	643	768
33700	293	489	645	770
33800	294	490	646	772
33900	295	491	648	774
34000	295	492	650	776
34100	296	493	651	777
34200	297	495	653	779
34300	298	496	654	781
34400	299	497	656	783
34500	299	498	657	785
34600	300	499	659	787
34700	301	501	660	789
34800	302	502	662	791
34900	302	503	663	792
35000	303	504	665	794
35100	304	505	667	796
35200	305	507	668	798
35300	305	508	670	800
35400	306	509	671	802
35500	307	510	673	804
35600	308	511	674	806
35700	309	513	676	807
35800	309	514	677	809
35900	310	515	679	811
36000	311	516	681	813
36100	312	517	682	815
36200	313	519	684	817
36300	313	520	685	819
36400	314	521	687	821
36500	315	522	689	823
36600	316	524	690	825
36700	317	525	692	827
36800	317	526	693	829
36900	318	527	695	831
37000	319	529	697	833
37100	320	530	698	835
37200	321	531	700	837
37300	321	532	701	838
37400	322	534	703	840
37500	323	535	705	842
37600	324	536	706	844
37700	325	537	708	846
37800	325	539	709	848
37900	326	540	711	850
38000	327	541	713	852
38100	328	542	714	854
38200	329	544	716	856
38300	329	545	717	858
38400	330	546	719	860
38500	331	547	721	862
38600	332	549	722	864
38700	333	550	724	866
38800	333	551	725	868
38900	334	552	727	870
39000	335	554	729	872
39100	336	555	730	874
39200	337	556	732	876
39300	337	557	734	877
39400	338	559	735	879
39500	339	560	737	881
39600	340	561	738	883
39700	341	562	740	885
39800	341	564	742	887
39900	342	565	743	889
40000	343	566	745	891
40100	344	568	746	893
40200	345	569	748	895
40300	346	570	750	897
40400	346	571	751	899
40500	347	573	753	901
40600	348	574	755	903
40700	349	575	756	905
40800	350	577	758	907
40900	351	578	760	909
41000	351	579	761	911
41100	352	581	763	913
41200	353	582	765	915
41300	354	583	766	917
41400	355	584	768	918
41500	356	586	770	920
41600	356	587	771	922
41700	357	588	773	924
41800	358	590	775	926
41900	359	591	776	928
42000	360	592	778	930
42100	361	593	780	932
42200	361	595	781	934
42300	362	596	783	936
42400	363	597	785	938
42500	364	599	786	940
42600	365	600	788	942
42700	366	601	790	944
42800	366	603	791	946
42900	367	604	793	948
43000	368	605	795	950
43100	369	606	796	952
43200	370	608	798	954
43300	371	609	800	956
43400	371	610	801	958
43500	372	612	803	960
43600	373	613	805	962
43700	374	614	806	964
43800	375	615	808	966
43900	376	617	810	968
44000	376	618	811	970
44100	377	619	813	972
44200	378	621	815	974
44300	379	622	816	976
44400	380	623	818	978
44500	381	625	820	979
44600	381	626	821	981
44700	382	627	823	983
44800	383	628	825	985
44900	384	630	826	987
45000	385	631	828	989
45100	386	632	830	991
45200	386	634	831	993
45300	387	635	833	995
45400	388	636	835	997
45500	389	638	836	999
45600	390	639	838	1001
45700	391	640	840	1003
45800	391	641	841	1005
45900	392	643	843	1007
46000	393	644	845	1009
46100	394	645	846	1011
46200	395	647	848	1013
46300	396	648	850	1015
46400	396	649	851	1017
46500	397	650	853	1019
46600	398	652	855	1021
46700	399	653	856	1023
46800	400	654	858	1025
46900	401	656	860	1027
47000	401	657	861	1029
47100	402	658	863	1031
47200	403	660	865	1033
47300	404	661	866	1035
47400	405	662	868	1037
47500	406	663	870	1039
47600	406	665	871	1041
47700	407	666	873	1042
47800	408	667	875	1044
47900	409	669	876	1046
48000	410	670	878	1048
48100	411	671	880	1050
48200	411	672	881	1052
48300	412	674	883	1054
48400	413	675	885	1056
48500	414	676	886	1058
48600	415	678	888	1060
48700	416	679	890	1062
48800	416	680	891	1064
48900	417	682	893	1066
49000	418	683	895	1068

Income/Revenu ($)	Monthly Award/Paiement mensuel ($) No. of Children/N^bre d'enfants			
	1	2	3	4
49100	419	684	896	1070
49200	420	685	898	1072
49300	421	687	900	1074
49400	421	688	901	1076
49500	422	689	903	1078
49600	423	691	905	1080
49700	424	692	906	1082
49800	425	693	908	1084
49900	426	695	910	1086
50000	426	696	911	1088
50100	427	697	913	1090
50200	428	698	915	1092
50300	429	700	916	1094
50400	430	701	918	1096
50500	431	702	920	1098
50600	431	704	921	1100
50700	432	705	923	1102
50800	433	706	925	1103
50900	434	707	926	1105
51000	435	709	928	1107
51100	436	710	930	1109
51200	436	711	931	1111
51300	437	713	933	1113
51400	438	714	935	1115
51500	439	715	936	1117
51600	440	717	938	1119
51700	441	718	940	1121
51800	441	719	941	1123
51900	442	720	943	1125
52000	443	722	945	1127
52100	444	723	946	1129
52200	445	724	948	1131
52300	445	726	950	1133
52400	446	727	951	1135
52500	447	728	953	1137
52600	448	729	955	1139
52700	449	731	956	1141
52800	450	732	958	1143
52900	450	733	960	1145
53000	451	735	961	1147
53100	452	735	963	1149
53200	453	737	965	1151
53300	454	739	966	1153
53400	455	740	968	1155
53500	455	741	970	1157
53600	456	742	971	1159
53700	457	744	973	1161
53800	458	745	975	1163
53900	459	746	976	1165
54000	460	748	978	1166
54100	460	749	980	1168
54200	461	750	981	1170
54300	462	752	983	1172

Income/Revenu ($)	Monthly Award/Paiement mensuel ($) No. of Children/N^bre d'enfants			
	1	2	3	4
54400	463	753	985	1174
54500	464	754	986	1176
54600	465	755	988	1178
54700	465	757	990	1180
54800	466	758	991	1182
54900	467	759	993	1184
55000	468	761	995	1186
55100	469	762	996	1188
55200	470	763	998	1190
55300	470	764	1000	1192
55400	471	766	1001	1194
55500	472	767	1003	1196
55600	473	768	1005	1198
55700	474	770	1006	1200
55800	475	771	1008	1202
55900	475	772	1009	1204
56000	476	773	1011	1205
56100	477	774	1012	1207
56200	477	775	1014	1209
56300	478	776	1015	1211
56400	479	777	1017	1212
56500	479	779	1018	1214
56600	480	780	1020	1216
56700	480	781	1021	1218
56800	481	782	1022	1219
56900	482	783	1024	1221
57000	482	784	1025	1223
57100	483	785	1027	1225
57200	484	786	1028	1226
57300	484	787	1030	1228
57400	485	788	1031	1230
57500	486	789	1033	1231
57600	486	791	1034	1233
57700	487	792	1035	1235
57800	487	793	1037	1237
57900	488	794	1038	1238
58000	489	795	1040	1240
58100	489	796	1041	1242
58200	490	797	1043	1244
58300	491	798	1044	1245
58400	491	799	1046	1247
58500	492	800	1047	1249
58600	493	801	1048	1251
58700	493	802	1050	1252
58800	494	804	1051	1254
58900	494	805	1053	1256
59000	495	806	1054	1258
59100	496	807	1056	1259
59200	496	808	1057	1261
59300	497	809	1058	1263
59400	497	810	1060	1264
59500	498	811	1061	1266
59600	499	812	1062	1267

Income/Revenu ($)	Monthly Award/Paiement mensuel ($) No. of Children/N^bre d'enfants			
	1	2	3	4
59700	499	813	1064	1269
59800	500	814	1065	1270
59900	500	815	1066	1272
60000	501	816	1067	1273
60100	501	817	1069	1275
60200	502	817	1070	1277
60300	502	818	1071	1278
60400	503	819	1073	1280
60500	504	820	1074	1281
60600	504	821	1075	1283
60700	505	822	1076	1284
60800	506	823	1078	1286
60900	506	824	1079	1287
61000	507	825	1080	1289
61100	508	826	1082	1291
61200	509	827	1083	1292
61300	509	828	1084	1294
61400	510	829	1085	1295
61500	511	830	1087	1297
61600	511	831	1088	1298
61700	512	832	1089	1300
61800	513	833	1091	1301
61900	514	834	1092	1303
62000	514	835	1093	1305
62100	515	837	1094	1306
62200	516	838	1096	1308
62300	516	839	1097	1309
62400	517	840	1098	1311
62500	518	841	1100	1312
62600	519	842	1101	1314
62700	519	843	1102	1316
62800	520	844	1104	1317
62900	521	845	1105	1319
63000	521	846	1106	1320
63100	522	848	1108	1322
63200	523	849	1109	1323
63300	523	850	1111	1325
63400	524	851	1112	1326
63500	525	852	1113	1328
63600	525	853	1115	1329
63700	526	854	1116	1331
63800	527	855	1117	1332
63900	527	856	1119	1334
64000	528	857	1120	1335
64100	529	858	1121	1337
64200	529	859	1123	1339
64300	530	860	1124	1340
64400	531	861	1125	1342
64500	531	862	1127	1343
64600	532	863	1128	1345
64700	532	864	1129	1347
64800	533	865	1131	1348
64900	534	866	1132	1350

Income/Revenu ($)	Monthly Award/Paiement mensuel ($) No. of Children/N^bre d'enfants			
	1	2	3	4
65000	534	867	1133	1351
65100	535	868	1135	1353
65200	536	869	1136	1355
65300	536	870	1137	1356
65400	537	871	1139	1358
65500	538	872	1140	1359
65600	538	873	1141	1361
65700	539	874	1143	1362
65800	539	875	1144	1364
65900	540	876	1145	1366
66000	541	877	1147	1367
66100	541	878	1148	1369
66200	542	879	1149	1370
66300	543	881	1151	1372
66400	543	882	1152	1374
66500	544	883	1153	1375
66600	545	884	1155	1377
66700	545	885	1156	1378
66800	546	886	1158	1380
66900	547	887	1159	1382
67000	547	888	1160	1383
67100	548	889	1162	1385
67200	549	890	1163	1387
67300	549	891	1164	1388
67400	550	892	1166	1390
67500	551	893	1167	1391
67600	551	894	1169	1393
67700	552	895	1170	1395
67800	553	896	1171	1396
67900	553	897	1173	1398
68000	554	899	1174	1399
68100	555	900	1175	1401
68200	556	901	1177	1403
68300	556	902	1178	1404
68400	557	903	1180	1406
68500	558	904	1181	1408
68600	558	905	1182	1409
68700	559	906	1184	1411
68800	559	907	1185	1412
68900	560	908	1186	1414
69000	561	909	1188	1416
69100	562	910	1189	1417
69200	562	911	1191	1419
69300	563	912	1192	1421
69400	564	914	1193	1422
69500	564	915	1195	1424
69600	565	916	1196	1425
69700	566	917	1197	1427
69800	567	918	1199	1429
69900	567	919	1200	1430
70000	568	920	1202	1432
70100	569	921	1203	1434
70200	569	922	1204	1435

Income/ Revenu ($)	Monthly Award/ Palement mensuel ($) No. of Children/ Nbre d'enfants				Income/ Revenu ($)	Monthly Award/ Palement mensuel ($) No. of Children/ Nbre d'enfants				Income/ Revenu ($)	Monthly Award/ Palement mensuel ($) No. of Children/ Nbre d'enfants				Income/ Revenu ($)	Monthly Award/ Palement mensuel ($) No. of Children/ Nbre d'enfants			
	1	2	3	4		1	2	3	4		1	2	3	4		1	2	3	4
70300	570	923	1206	1437	75600	606	980	1278	1523	80900	643	1036	1351	1609	86200	673	1086	1416	1686
70400	571	924	1207	1438	75700	607	981	1280	1524	81000	643	1037	1353	1611	86300	673	1087	1417	1688
70500	571	925	1208	1440	75800	608	982	1281	1526	81100	644	1039	1354	1612	86400	674	1088	1418	1689
70600	572	926	1210	1442	75900	608	983	1283	1528	81200	645	1040	1355	1614	86500	675	1089	1420	1691
70700	573	927	1211	1443	76000	609	984	1284	1529	81300	645	1040	1357	1615	86600	675	1090	1421	1692
70800	573	928	1213	1445	76100	610	985	1285	1531	81400	646	1041	1358	1617	86700	676	1091	1422	1694
70900	574	930	1214	1447	76200	610	986	1287	1533	81500	646	1042	1359	1618	86800	676	1091	1423	1695
71000	575	931	1215	1448	76300	611	987	1288	1534	81600	647	1043	1360	1619	86900	677	1092	1425	1697
71100	575	932	1217	1450	76400	612	988	1289	1536	81700	647	1044	1361	1621	87000	678	1093	1426	1698
71200	576	933	1218	1451	76500	613	989	1291	1537	81800	648	1045	1362	1622	87100	678	1094	1427	1700
71300	577	934	1219	1453	76600	613	990	1292	1539	81900	648	1046	1364	1624	87200	679	1095	1429	1701
71400	578	935	1221	1455	76700	614	992	1294	1541	82000	649	1047	1365	1625	87300	680	1096	1430	1703
71500	578	936	1222	1456	76800	615	993	1295	1542	82100	649	1047	1366	1626	87400	680	1097	1431	1704
71600	579	937	1224	1458	76900	615	994	1296	1544	82200	650	1048	1367	1628	87500	681	1098	1432	1706
71700	580	938	1225	1460	77000	616	995	1298	1546	82300	650	1049	1368	1629	87600	682	1099	1434	1707
71800	580	939	1226	1461	77100	617	996	1299	1547	82400	651	1050	1369	1631	87700	682	1100	1435	1709
71900	581	940	1228	1463	77200	617	997	1300	1549	82500	651	1051	1371	1632	87800	683	1101	1436	1710
72000	582	941	1229	1464	77300	618	998	1302	1550	82600	652	1052	1372	1634	87900	684	1102	1437	1712
72100	582	942	1230	1466	77400	619	999	1303	1552	82700	652	1053	1373	1635	88000	684	1103	1439	1713
72200	583	943	1232	1468	77500	619	1000	1305	1554	82800	653	1054	1374	1636	88100	685	1104	1440	1715
72300	584	945	1233	1469	77600	620	1001	1306	1555	82900	653	1054	1375	1638	88200	685	1105	1441	1716
72400	584	946	1235	1471	77700	621	1002	1307	1557	83000	654	1055	1376	1639	88300	686	1106	1443	1718
72500	585	947	1236	1473	77800	621	1003	1309	1559	83100	654	1056	1378	1641	88400	687	1107	1444	1719
72600	586	948	1237	1474	77900	622	1004	1310	1560	83200	655	1057	1379	1642	88500	687	1108	1445	1721
72700	586	949	1239	1476	78000	623	1005	1311	1562	83300	656	1058	1380	1643	88600	688	1109	1446	1722
72800	587	950	1240	1477	78100	624	1006	1313	1563	83400	656	1059	1381	1645	88700	689	1110	1448	1724
72900	588	951	1241	1479	78200	624	1008	1314	1565	83500	657	1060	1382	1646	88800	689	1111	1449	1725
73000	589	952	1243	1481	78300	625	1009	1316	1567	83600	657	1061	1383	1648	88900	690	1112	1450	1727
73100	589	953	1244	1482	78400	626	1010	1317	1568	83700	658	1062	1385	1649	89000	691	1113	1451	1728
73200	590	954	1246	1484	78500	626	1011	1318	1570	83800	658	1062	1386	1650	89100	691	1114	1453	1730
73300	591	955	1247	1486	78600	627	1012	1320	1572	83900	659	1063	1387	1652	89200	692	1115	1454	1731
73400	591	956	1248	1487	78700	628	1013	1321	1573	84000	659	1064	1388	1653	89300	692	1116	1455	1733
73500	592	957	1250	1489	78800	628	1014	1322	1575	84100	660	1065	1389	1655	89400	693	1117	1457	1734
73600	593	958	1251	1490	78900	629	1015	1324	1576	84200	660	1066	1391	1656	89500	694	1118	1458	1736
73700	593	959	1252	1492	79000	630	1016	1325	1578	84300	661	1067	1392	1658	89600	694	1119	1459	1737
73800	594	961	1254	1494	79100	630	1017	1327	1580	84400	661	1068	1393	1659	89700	695	1120	1460	1739
73900	595	962	1255	1495	79200	631	1018	1328	1581	84500	662	1069	1394	1661	89800	696	1121	1462	1740
74000	595	963	1256	1497	79300	632	1019	1329	1583	84600	662	1070	1395	1662	89900	696	1122	1463	1742
74100	596	964	1258	1499	79400	632	1020	1331	1585	84700	663	1071	1397	1664	90000	697	1123	1464	1743
74200	597	965	1259	1500	79500	633	1021	1332	1586	84800	664	1072	1398	1665	90100	698	1124	1465	1745
74300	597	966	1261	1502	79600	634	1022	1333	1588	84900	664	1073	1399	1667	90200	698	1125	1467	1746
74400	598	967	1262	1503	79700	635	1024	1335	1589	85000	665	1074	1401	1668	90300	699	1126	1468	1748
74500	599	968	1263	1505	79800	635	1025	1336	1591	85100	666	1075	1402	1670	90400	699	1127	1469	1749
74600	600	969	1265	1507	79900	636	1026	1338	1593	85200	666	1076	1403	1671	90500	700	1128	1471	1751
74700	600	970	1266	1508	80000	637	1027	1339	1594	85300	667	1077	1404	1673	90600	701	1129	1472	1752
74800	601	971	1267	1510	80100	637	1028	1340	1596	85400	668	1078	1406	1674	90700	701	1130	1473	1754
74900	602	972	1269	1512	80200	638	1029	1342	1598	85500	668	1079	1407	1676	90800	702	1131	1474	1755
75000	602	973	1270	1513	80300	639	1030	1343	1599	85600	669	1080	1408	1677	90900	703	1132	1476	1757
75100	603	974	1272	1515	80400	639	1031	1344	1601	85700	669	1081	1409	1679	91000	703	1133	1477	1758
75200	604	975	1273	1516	80500	640	1032	1346	1602	85800	670	1082	1411	1680	91100	704	1134	1478	1760
75300	604	977	1274	1518	80600	641	1033	1347	1604	85900	671	1083	1412	1682	91200	705	1135	1480	1761
75400	605	978	1276	1520	80700	641	1034	1349	1606	86000	671	1084	1413	1683	91300	705	1136	1481	1763
75500	606	979	1277	1521	80800	642	1035	1350	1607	86100	672	1085	1415	1685	91400	706	1137	1482	1764

Monthly Award/ Paiement mensuel ($) — No. of Children/ Nᵇʳᵉ d'enfants

Income/ Revenu ($)	1	2	3	4
91500	706	1138	1483	1766
91600	707	1139	1485	1767
91700	708	1140	1486	1769
91800	708	1141	1487	1770
91900	709	1142	1488	1772
92000	710	1143	1490	1773
92100	710	1144	1491	1775
92200	711	1145	1492	1776
92300	712	1146	1494	1778
92400	712	1147	1495	1779
92500	713	1148	1496	1781
92600	713	1149	1497	1782
92700	714	1150	1499	1784
92800	715	1151	1500	1785
92900	715	1152	1501	1787
93000	716	1153	1502	1788
93100	717	1154	1504	1790
93200	717	1155	1505	1791
93300	718	1156	1506	1793
93400	719	1157	1508	1794
93500	719	1158	1509	1796
93600	720	1159	1510	1797
93700	720	1160	1511	1799
93800	721	1161	1513	1800
93900	722	1162	1514	1802
94000	722	1163	1515	1803
94100	723	1164	1516	1805
94200	724	1165	1518	1806
94300	724	1166	1519	1808
94400	725	1167	1520	1809
94500	726	1168	1522	1811
94600	726	1169	1523	1812
94700	727	1170	1524	1814
94800	727	1171	1525	1815
94900	728	1172	1527	1817
95000	729	1173	1528	1818
95100	729	1174	1529	1820
95200	730	1175	1530	1821
95300	731	1176	1532	1823
95400	731	1177	1533	1825
95500	732	1178	1534	1826
95600	733	1179	1536	1828
95700	733	1180	1537	1829
95800	734	1181	1538	1831
95900	734	1182	1539	1832
96000	735	1183	1541	1834
96100	736	1184	1542	1835
96200	736	1185	1543	1837
96300	737	1186	1544	1838
96400	737	1187	1546	1840
96500	738	1188	1547	1841
96600	738	1189	1548	1843
96700	739	1190	1550	1844

Income/ Revenu ($)	1	2	3	4
96800	740	1191	1551	1846
96900	741	1191	1552	1847
97000	741	1192	1553	1849
97100	742	1193	1555	1850
97200	743	1194	1556	1852
97300	743	1195	1557	1853
97400	744	1195	1558	1855
97500	745	1197	1560	1855
97600	745	1198	1561	1858
97700	746	1199	1562	1859
97800	747	1200	1564	1861
97900	747	1201	1565	1862
98000	748	1202	1566	1864
98100	748	1203	1567	1865
98200	749	1204	1569	1867
98300	750	1205	1570	1868
98400	750	1206	1571	1870
98500	751	1207	1572	1871
98600	752	1208	1574	1873
98700	752	1209	1575	1874
98800	753	1210	1576	1876
98900	754	1211	1578	1877
99000	754	1212	1579	1879
99100	755	1213	1580	1882
99200	755	1214	1581	1882
99300	756	1215	1583	1883
99400	757	1216	1584	1885
99500	757	1217	1585	1885
99600	758	1218	1586	1888
99700	759	1219	1588	1889
99800	759	1220	1589	1891
99900	760	1221	1590	1892
100000	761	1222	1592	1894
100100	761	1223	1593	1895
100200	762	1224	1594	1897
100300	762	1225	1595	1898
100400	763	1226	1597	1900
100500	764	1227	1598	1901
100600	764	1228	1599	1903
100700	765	1229	1600	1904
100800	766	1230	1602	1906
100900	766	1231	1603	1907
101000	767	1232	1604	1909
101100	768	1233	1606	1910
101200	768	1234	1607	1912
101300	769	1235	1608	1913
101400	769	1236	1609	1915
101500	770	1237	1611	1916
101600	770	1238	1612	1918
101700	771	1239	1613	1919
101800	771	1240	1614	1921
101900	772	1241	1616	1922
102000	773	1242	1617	1924

Income/ Revenu ($)	1	2	3	4
102100	774	1243	1618	1925
102200	775	1244	1620	1927
102300	775	1245	1621	1928
102400	776	1246	1622	1930
102500	776	1247	1623	1931
102600	777	1248	1625	1933
102700	778	1249	1626	1934
102800	778	1250	1627	1936
102900	779	1251	1628	1937
103000	780	1252	1630	1939
103100	780	1253	1631	1940
103200	781	1254	1632	1942
103300	782	1255	1634	1943
103400	782	1256	1635	1945
103500	783	1257	1636	1946
103600	783	1258	1637	1948
103700	784	1259	1639	1949
103800	785	1260	1640	1951
103900	785	1261	1641	1952
104000	786	1262	1642	1954
104100	787	1263	1644	1955
104200	787	1264	1645	1957
104300	788	1265	1646	1958
104400	789	1266	1648	1960
104500	789	1267	1649	1961
104600	790	1268	1650	1963
104700	790	1269	1651	1964
104800	791	1270	1653	1966
104900	792	1271	1654	1967
105000	792	1272	1655	1969
105100	793	1273	1656	1970
105200	794	1274	1658	1972
105300	794	1275	1659	1973
105400	795	1276	1660	1975
105500	796	1277	1662	1976
105600	796	1278	1663	1978
105700	797	1279	1664	1979
105800	797	1280	1665	1981
105900	798	1281	1667	1982
106000	799	1282	1668	1984
106100	799	1283	1669	1986
106200	800	1284	1670	1987
106300	801	1285	1672	1988
106400	801	1286	1673	1990
106500	802	1287	1674	1992
106600	803	1288	1676	1993
106700	803	1289	1677	1995
106800	804	1290	1678	1996
106900	804	1291	1679	1998
107000	805	1292	1681	1999
107100	806	1292	1682	2001
107200	806	1293	1683	2002
107300	807	1294	1684	2004

Income/ Revenu ($)	1	2	3	4
107400	808	1295	1686	2005
107500	808	1296	1687	2007
107600	809	1297	1688	2008
107700	810	1298	1690	2010
107800	810	1299	1691	2011
107900	811	1300	1692	2013
108000	811	1301	1693	2014
108100	812	1302	1695	2016
108200	813	1303	1696	2017
108300	813	1304	1697	2019
108400	814	1305	1698	2020
108500	815	1306	1700	2022
108600	815	1307	1701	2023
108700	816	1308	1702	2025
108800	817	1309	1704	2026
108900	817	1310	1705	2028
109000	818	1311	1706	2029
109100	818	1312	1707	2031
109200	819	1313	1709	2032
109300	820	1314	1710	2034
109400	820	1315	1711	2035
109500	821	1316	1712	2037
109600	822	1317	1714	2038
109700	822	1318	1715	2040
109800	823	1319	1716	2041
109900	824	1320	1718	2043
110000	824	1321	1719	2044
110100	825	1322	1720	2046
110200	825	1323	1721	2047
110300	826	1324	1723	2049
110400	827	1325	1724	2051
110500	827	1326	1725	2052
110600	828	1327	1726	2053
110700	829	1328	1728	2055
110800	829	1329	1729	2056
110900	830	1330	1730	2058
111000	831	1331	1732	2059
111100	831	1332	1733	2061
111200	832	1333	1734	2062
111300	832	1334	1735	2064
111400	833	1335	1737	2065
111500	833	1336	1738	2067
111600	834	1337	1739	2068
111700	835	1338	1740	2070
111800	836	1339	1742	2071
111900	836	1340	1743	2073
112000	837	1341	1744	2074
112100	838	1342	1746	2076
112200	838	1343	1747	2077
112300	839	1344	1748	2079
112400	839	1345	1749	2080
112500	840	1346	1751	2082
112600	841	1347	1752	2083

143

Income/ Revenu ($)	Monthly Award/ Paiement mensuel ($) No. of Children/ N^bre d'enfants				Income/ Revenu ($)	Monthly Award/ Paiement mensuel ($) No. of Children/ N^bre d'enfants				Income/ Revenu ($)	Monthly Award/ Paiement mensuel ($) No. of Children/ N^bre d'enfants				Income/ Revenu ($)	Monthly Award/ Paiement mensuel ($) No. of Children/ N^bre d'enfants			
	1	2	3	4		1	2	3	4		1	2	3	4		1	2	3	4
112700	841	1348	1753	2085	118000	875	1400	1821	2165	123300	909	1453	1888	2244	128600	943	1505	1956	2324
112800	842	1349	1754	2086	118100	876	1401	1822	2166	123400	909	1454	1889	2246	128700	943	1506	1957	2326
112900	843	1350	1756	2088	118200	876	1402	1823	2168	123500	910	1455	1891	2247	128800	944	1507	1958	2327
113000	843	1351	1757	2089	118300	877	1403	1824	2169	123600	911	1456	1892	2249	128900	944	1508	1959	2329
113100	844	1352	1758	2091	118400	878	1404	1826	2171	123700	911	1457	1893	2250	129000	945	1509	1961	2330
113200	845	1353	1760	2092	118500	878	1405	1827	2172	123800	912	1458	1895	2252	129100	946	1510	1962	2332
113300	845	1354	1761	2094	118600	879	1406	1828	2174	123900	913	1459	1896	2253	129200	946	1511	1963	2333
113400	846	1355	1762	2095	118700	880	1407	1830	2175	124000	913	1460	1897	2255	129300	947	1512	1965	2335
113500	846	1356	1763	2097	118800	880	1408	1831	2177	124100	914	1461	1898	2256	129400	948	1513	1966	2336
113600	847	1357	1765	2098	118900	881	1409	1832	2178	124200	915	1462	1900	2258	129500	948	1514	1967	2338
113700	848	1358	1766	2100	119000	881	1410	1833	2180	124300	915	1463	1901	2259	129600	949	1515	1968	2339
113800	848	1359	1767	2101	119100	882	1411	1835	2181	124400	916	1464	1902	2261	129700	950	1516	1970	2341
113900	849	1360	1768	2103	119200	883	1412	1836	2183	124500	916	1465	1903	2262	129800	950	1517	1971	2342
114000	850	1361	1770	2104	119300	883	1413	1837	2184	124600	917	1466	1905	2264	129900	951	1518	1972	2344
114100	850	1362	1771	2106	119400	884	1414	1838	2186	124700	918	1467	1906	2265	130000	951	1519	1973	2345
114200	851	1363	1772	2107	119500	885	1415	1840	2187	124800	918	1468	1907	2267	130100	952	1520	1975	2347
114300	852	1364	1774	2109	119600	885	1416	1841	2189	124900	919	1469	1909	2268	130200	953	1521	1976	2348
114400	852	1365	1775	2110	119700	886	1417	1842	2190	125000	920	1470	1910	2270	130300	953	1522	1977	2350
114500	853	1366	1776	2112	119800	887	1418	1844	2192	125100	920	1471	1911	2271	130400	954	1523	1979	2351
114600	853	1367	1777	2113	119900	887	1419	1845	2193	125200	921	1472	1912	2273	130500	955	1524	1980	2353
114700	854	1368	1779	2115	120000	888	1420	1846	2195	125300	922	1473	1914	2274	130600	955	1525	1981	2354
114800	855	1369	1780	2116	120100	888	1421	1847	2196	125400	922	1474	1915	2276	130700	956	1526	1982	2356
114900	855	1370	1781	2118	120200	889	1422	1849	2198	125500	923	1475	1916	2277	130800	957	1527	1984	2357
115000	856	1371	1782	2119	120300	890	1423	1850	2199	125600	923	1476	1917	2279	130900	957	1528	1985	2359
115100	857	1372	1784	2121	120400	890	1424	1851	2201	125700	924	1477	1919	2280	131000	958	1529	1986	2360
115200	857	1373	1785	2122	120500	891	1425	1853	2202	125800	925	1478	1920	2282	131100	958	1530	1987	2362
115300	858	1374	1786	2124	120600	892	1426	1854	2204	125900	925	1479	1921	2283	131200	959	1531	1989	2363
115400	859	1375	1788	2125	120700	892	1427	1855	2205	126000	926	1480	1923	2285	131300	960	1532	1990	2365
115500	859	1376	1789	2127	120800	893	1428	1856	2207	126100	927	1481	1924	2286	131400	960	1533	1991	2366
115600	860	1377	1790	2128	120900	894	1429	1858	2208	126200	927	1482	1925	2288	131500	961	1534	1993	2368
115700	860	1378	1791	2130	121000	894	1430	1859	2210	126300	928	1483	1926	2289	131600	962	1535	1994	2369
115800	861	1379	1793	2131	121100	895	1431	1860	2211	126400	929	1484	1928	2291	131700	962	1536	1995	2371
115900	862	1380	1794	2133	121200	895	1432	1861	2213	126500	929	1485	1929	2292	131800	963	1537	1996	2372
116000	862	1381	1795	2134	121300	896	1433	1863	2214	126600	930	1486	1930	2294	131900	964	1538	1998	2374
116100	863	1382	1796	2136	121400	897	1434	1864	2216	126700	930	1487	1931	2295	132000	964	1539	1999	2375
116200	864	1383	1798	2137	121500	897	1435	1865	2217	126800	931	1488	1933	2297	132100	965	1540	2000	2377
116300	864	1384	1799	2139	121600	898	1436	1867	2219	126900	932	1489	1934	2298	132200	965	1541	2001	2378
116400	865	1385	1800	2140	121700	899	1437	1868	2220	127000	932	1490	1935	2300	132300	966	1542	2003	2380
116500	866	1386	1802	2142	121800	899	1438	1869	2222	127100	933	1491	1937	2301	132400	967	1543	2004	2381
116600	866	1387	1803	2143	121900	900	1439	1870	2223	127200	934	1492	1938	2303	132500	967	1544	2005	2383
116700	867	1388	1804	2145	122000	901	1440	1872	2225	127300	934	1493	1939	2304	132600	968	1545	2007	2384
116800	867	1389	1805	2146	122100	901	1441	1873	2226	127400	935	1493	1941	2306	132700	969	1546	2008	2386
116900	868	1390	1807	2148	122200	902	1442	1874	2228	127500	936	1494	1942	2307	132800	969	1547	2009	2387
117000	869	1391	1808	2149	122300	902	1443	1875	2229	127600	936	1495	1943	2309	132900	970	1548	2010	2389
117100	869	1392	1809	2151	122400	903	1444	1877	2231	127700	937	1496	1944	2310	133000	971	1549	2012	2391
117200	870	1392	1810	2152	122500	904	1445	1878	2232	127800	937	1497	1945	2312	133100	971	1550	2013	2392
117300	871	1393	1812	2154	122600	904	1446	1879	2234	127900	938	1498	1947	2313	133200	972	1551	2014	2394
117400	871	1394	1813	2155	122700	905	1447	1881	2235	128000	939	1499	1948	2315	133300	972	1552	2015	2395
117500	872	1395	1814	2157	122800	906	1448	1882	2237	128100	939	1500	1949	2316	133400	973	1553	2017	2397
117600	873	1396	1816	2159	122900	906	1449	1883	2238	128200	540	1501	1951	2318	133500	973	1554	2018	2398
117700	873	1397	1817	2160	123000	907	1450	1884	2240	128300	941	1502	1952	2319	133600	974	1555	2019	2400
117800	874	1398	1818	2162	123100	908	1451	1886	2241	128400	941	1503	1953	2321	133700	975	1556	2020	2401
117900	874	1399	1819	2163	123200	908	1452	1887	2243	128500	542	1504	1954	2322	133800	976	1557	2022	2403

144

Income/Revenu ($)	Monthly Award/Paiement mensuel ($) No. of Children/Nᵇʳᵉ d'enfants			
	1	2	3	4
3900	976	1558	2023	2404
4000	977	1559	2024	2405
4100	978	1560	2026	2407
4200	978	1561	2027	2408
4300	979	1562	2028	2410
4400	979	1563	2029	2411
4500	980	1564	2031	2413
4600	981	1565	2032	2414
4700	981	1566	2033	2416
4800	982	1567	2035	2417
4900	983	1568	2036	2419
5000	983	1569	2037	2420
5100	984	1570	2038	2422
5200	985	1571	2040	2423
5300	985	1572	2041	2425
5400	986	1573	2042	2426
5500	986	1574	2043	2428
5600	987	1575	2045	2429
5700	988	1576	2046	2431
5800	988	1577	2047	2432
5900	989	1578	2049	2434
6000	990	1579	2050	2435
6100	990	1580	2051	2437
6200	991	1581	2052	2438
6300	992	1582	2054	2440
6400	992	1583	2055	2441
6500	993	1584	2056	2443
6600	993	1585	2057	2444
6700	994	1586	2059	2446
6800	995	1587	2060	2447
6900	995	1588	2061	2449
7000	996	1589	2063	2450
7100	997	1590	2064	2452
7200	997	1591	2065	2453
7300	998	1592	2066	2455
7400	999	1593	2068	2456
7500	999	1593	2069	2458
7600	1000	1594	2070	2459
7700	1000	1595	2071	2461
7800	1001	1596	2073	2462
7900	1002	1597	2074	2464

Income/Revenu ($)	Monthly Award/Paiement mensuel ($) No. of Children/Nᵇʳᵉ d'enfants			
	1	2	3	4
138000	1002	1598	2075	2465
138100	1003	1599	2077	2467
138200	1004	1600	2078	2468
138300	1004	1601	2079	2470
138400	1005	1602	2080	2471
138500	1006	1603	2082	2473
138600	1006	1604	2083	2474
138700	1007	1605	2084	2476
138800	1007	1606	2085	2477
138900	1008	1607	2087	2479
139000	1009	1608	2088	2480
139100	1009	1609	2089	2482
139200	1010	1610	2091	2483
139300	1011	1611	2092	2485
139400	1011	1612	2093	2486
139500	1012	1613	2094	2488
139600	1013	1614	2096	2489
139700	1013	1615	2097	2491
139800	1014	1616	2098	2493
139900	1014	1617	2099	2494
140000	1015	1618	2101	2496
140100	1016	1619	2102	2497
140200	1016	1620	2103	2499
140300	1017	1621	2105	2500
140400	1018	1622	2106	2502
140500	1018	1623	2107	2503
140600	1019	1624	2108	2505
140700	1020	1625	2110	2506
140800	1020	1626	2111	2508
140900	1021	1627	2112	2509
141000	1021	1628	2113	2511
141100	1022	1629	2115	2512
141200	1023	1630	2116	2514
141300	1023	1631	2117	2515
141400	1024	1632	2119	2517
141500	1025	1633	2120	2518
141600	1025	1634	2121	2520
141700	1026	1635	2122	2521
141800	1027	1636	2124	2523
141900	1027	1637	2125	2524
142000	1028	1638	2126	2526

Income/Revenu ($)	Monthly Award/Paiement mensuel ($) No. of Children/Nᵇʳᵉ d'enfants			
	1	2	3	4
142100	1028	1639	2127	2527
142200	1029	1640	2129	2529
142300	1030	1641	2130	2530
142400	1030	1642	2131	2532
142500	1031	1643	2133	2533
142600	1032	1644	2134	2535
142700	1032	1645	2135	2536
142800	1033	1646	2136	2538
142900	1034	1647	2138	2539
143000	1034	1648	2139	2541
143100	1035	1649	2140	2542
143200	1035	1650	2141	2544
143300	1036	1651	2143	2545
143400	1037	1652	2144	2547
143500	1037	1653	2145	2548
143600	1038	1654	2147	2550
143700	1039	1655	2148	2551
143800	1039	1656	2149	2553
143900	1040	1657	2150	2554
144000	1041	1658	2152	2556
144100	1041	1659	2153	2557
144200	1042	1660	2154	2559
144300	1042	1661	2155	2560
144400	1043	1662	2157	2562
144500	1044	1663	2158	2563
144600	1044	1664	2159	2565
144700	1045	1665	2161	2566
144800	1046	1666	2162	2568
144900	1046	1667	2163	2569
145000	1047	1668	2164	2571
145100	1048	1669	2166	2572
145200	1048	1670	2167	2574
145300	1049	1671	2168	2575
145400	1049	1672	2169	2577
145500	1050	1673	2171	2578
145600	1050	1674	2172	2580
145700	1051	1675	2173	2581
145800	1052	1676	2175	2583
145900	1052	1677	2176	2584
146000	1053	1678	2177	2586
146100	1054	1679	2178	2587

Income/Revenu ($)	Monthly Award/Paiement mensuel ($) No. of Children/Nᵇʳᵉ d'enfants			
	1	2	3	4
146200	1055	1680	2180	2589
146300	1055	1681	2181	2590
146400	1056	1682	2182	2592
146500	1057	1683	2183	2593
146600	1057	1684	2185	2595
146700	1058	1685	2186	2596
146800	1058	1686	2187	2598
146900	1059	1687	2189	2599
147000	1060	1688	2190	2601
147100	1060	1689	2191	2602
147200	1061	1690	2192	2604
147300	1062	1691	2194	2605
147400	1062	1692	2195	2607
147500	1063	1693	2196	2608
147600	1064	1693	2197	2610
147700	1064	1694	2199	2611
147800	1065	1695	2200	2613
147900	1065	1696	2201	2614
148000	1066	1697	2203	2616
148100	1067	1698	2204	2617
148200	1067	1699	2205	2619
148300	1068	1700	2206	2620
148400	1069	1701	2208	2622
148500	1069	1702	2209	2623
148600	1070	1703	2210	2625
148700	1071	1704	2211	2626
148800	1071	1705	2213	2628
148900	1072	1706	2214	2629
149000	1072	1707	2215	2631
149100	1073	1708	2217	2632
149200	1074	1709	2218	2634
149300	1074	1710	2219	2635
149400	1075	1711	2220	2637
149500	1076	1712	2222	2638
149600	1076	1713	2223	2640
149700	1077	1714	2224	2641
149800	1078	1715	2226	2643
149900	1078	1716	2227	2644
150000	1079	1717	2228	2646

Income/Revenu ($)	Monthly Award/Paiement mensuel ($)			
	one child/un enfant	two children/deux enfants	three children/trois enfants	four children/quatre enfants
For Income over $150,000	1079 plus 0.64% of income over $150,000	1717 plus 0.99% of income over $150,000	2228 plus 1.27% of income over $150,000	2646 plus 1.50% of income over $150,000
Pour revenu passant 150 000$	1079 plus 0,64% du revenu dépassant 150 000$	1717 plus 0,99% du revenu dépassant 150 000$	2228 plus 1,27% du revenu dépassant 150 000$	2646 plus 1,50% du revenu dépassant 150 000$

If you have enjoyed this book and would like to receive a free catalogue of all Self-Counsel titles, please write to:

Self Counsel Press
1481 Charlotte Road
North Vancouver, BC V7J 1H1

Or visit us on the World Wide Web at *www.self-counsel.com*

Other titles in the Self-Counsel Legal Series:

Living Together Contract
Wills Guide for British Columbia
Have You Made Your Will? (forms)
Divorce Guide & Forms for British Columbia
If You Leave Me, Put It In Writing